Leadership for Low-Performing Schools

Leadership for Low-Performing Schools

A Step-by-Step Guide to the School Turnaround Process

DANIEL L. DUKE

ROWMAN & LITTLEFIELD
Lanham • Boulder • New York • London

Published by Rowman & Littlefield
A wholly owned subsidiary of The Rowman & Littlefield Publishing Group, Inc.
4501 Forbes Boulevard, Suite 200, Lanham, Maryland 20706
www.rowman.com

Unit A, Whitacre Mews, 26-34 Stannary Street, London SE11 4AB

British Library Cataloguing in Publication Information Available

Library of Congress Cataloging-in-Publication Data Available
ISBN: 978-1-4758-1024-0 (cloth : alk. paper)
ISBN: 978-1-4758-1025-7 (pbk : alk. paper)
ISBN: 978-1-4758-1026-4 (electronic)

∞™ The paper used in this publication meets the minimum requirements of American National Standard for Information Sciences—Permanence of Paper for Printed Library Materials, ANSI/NISO Z39.48-1992.

Printed in the United States of America

For Cheryl, Devan, and Noelle—
the lights and delights of my life

Contents

Introduction

Imagine that you've had a successful run as principal of a high-performing elementary school. Your superintendent asks you to take on the principalship of an elementary school in improvement status. You became an educator in order to help the most needy children, so you tell her that you're up to the challenge.

Your new school is the most diverse in the school system and one of the lowest performing. Barely half of the students who qualify for free and reduced price lunch passed the state tests in mathematics. The pass rate for African American students was 43 percent. Still, these figures represented improvements over the previous year. Achievement on the English tests, on the other hand, has been steadily slipping as the percentage of foreign-born students grows.

You spend the summer sizing up the problems that need to be addressed. First, the faculty clearly hasn't made the instructional adjustments necessary to address the needs of an increasingly diverse student body. Second, the school has suffered from a high turnover rate among teachers and administrators. Third, your predecessor's plans for improving student achievement lacked a clear focus.

What would you do to turn around this elementary school?

You require, of course, much more information before you can offer a tentative response. In the chapters to follow, you'll receive plenty of ideas about how to lead low-performing schools and make the achievement gains and organizational improvements on which so many young people depend. You also will learn how the principal of the above elementary school, as well as many other turnaround principals, made dramatic improvements in their schools.

It takes a special kind of person to lead a low-performing school toward success for all students. And a special brand of leadership. *Never-give-up leadership* is what I call it. The leadership needed to achieve school turnaround, I maintain, is qualitatively different from the leadership needed for other schools. To be sure, all principals need to know certain "basics," including education law, school finance, and principles of staff supervision. But there also are things *beyond* the conventional curriculum that must be mastered in order to tackle the challenges of reversing years of low achievement and then sustaining improvements over time. This book focuses on the things that lie beyond—the special knowledge, skills, beliefs, and understandings needed to turn around a low-performing school and keep it turned around.

LEADERS—CAUSE AND CURE

Once upon a time when student achievement failed to match expectations, the blame was placed squarely on the students themselves (Duke, 1978). Unsuccessful students must be unmotivated, careless, or just plain lazy. Over the years the responsibility for low achievement shifted to teachers. Lack of academic success had to be a function of inadequate instruction and lack of timely assistance. Then with the passage of the Elementary and Secondary Education Act in 1965, attention was directed from struggling students and inept teachers to the impact of poverty on academic performance. Schools with large percentages of students from disadvantaged homes received supplementary funds to purchase additional personnel and special services.

Since 1965 thinking about these challenging schools has evolved. So, too, has terminology. Once referred to as *high-needs schools*, they have come to be labeled *low-performing schools*. The shift from needs to performance is but one indication of the increasing focus on accountability, a focus symbolized by the passage of the No Child Left Behind Act in 2001. Another indication is the change in strategy from relying on supplementary funding with few strings attached to the implementation of sanctions for low performance.

Schools in which students consistently miss prescribed benchmarks face reconstitution and possible closure.

Prescriptions for school improvements also have evolved. Adding personnel and special services morphed into school restructuring, which then gave way to comprehensive school reform. The twenty-first century ushered in the era of school turnaround and a shift in expectations from "slow and steady" to "quick and dramatic" school improvement.

Throughout a half century of concern over academically challenged schools, one of the few constants has been school leadership. When the causes of low performance are diagnosed, fingers continue to point to ineffective principals. The predictable solution—find principals with the competence and commitment to lead the school turnaround process.

Today no greater challenge faces our society than improving the educational opportunities for millions of young people trapped in low-performing schools. Some observers believe that little can be done to save these schools and they consequently should be shuttered (Stuit, 2010). Perhaps a handful of schools do stand little chance of escaping the gravitational pull of failure, poverty, and bad reputation, but most low-performing schools are not beyond hope. There are too many successful turnarounds to warrant giving up. But even if there was just one success story, as Ron Edmonds (1982) noted years ago, it would prove that turnaround was possible. Recognition that at least one low-performing school has been turned around changes the question we must ask ourselves. Instead of asking, "Is it possible to turn around a low-performing school?" the question becomes, "What is preventing other schools from turning around?"

I have visited dozens of schools that have turned around and read about dozens more. In no case was the principal an ineffectual bystander. Principals, of course, do not turn around low-performing schools singlehandedly, but neither are schools turned around without a never-give-up principal.

To appreciate what is entailed in leading the school turnaround process, I find the metaphors of designer, architect, and builder useful. Designers create a vision for what is needed. In the case of a low-performing school, for example, the vision could be to restore a declining school to its previous level of academic success, or ensure that most students achieve acceptable pass rates on state tests, or create a totally different kind of school that better serves the needs of students.

Whatever design is chosen, a plan is required to move from conception to concreteness. That is the job of architects. They take general desires and convert them to specific details. Builders then take these details—the blueprints or plans—and make intentions tangible.

In the world of construction, different individuals are commissioned as designers, architects, and builders. An effective principal charged with turning around a low-performing school, however, needs to function in all three roles. This is just one reason why turnaround leadership requires special talents.

There are many other reasons. Just take a look at some of the responsibilities listed in an advertisement for a turnaround principal:

- Lead the implementation of strategies for improving student achievement;
- Lead teacher teams to create a coherent instructional program focused on state standards, higher order thinking skills, inclusion and differentiation;
- Observe, supervise, coach and evaluate all staff using a variety of techniques;
- Lead a data-driven instruction initiative using interim assessments for the development of instructional action plans in literacy, mathematics and science;
- Create a school infrastructure for materials management and scheduling. (Academy for Urban School Leadership, 2009)

The structures, processes, and practices that educators in high-performing schools take for granted are frequently absent in low-performing schools. These schools literally must be rebuilt from the ground up—another reason why I like the designer/architect/builder analogy.

WHAT YOU'LL FIND IN THIS BOOK

Leadership for Low-Performing Schools is organized to reflect the series of considerations and actions involved in turning around a struggling school. Before embarking on this journey, however, it is important to think about the special demands this process will make on the individual school leader. The first chapter examines some of the predictable challenges that turnaround principals face. The chapter goes on to identify what principals need to know about the process of change and change leadership in order to be effective.

One key to effective change leadership involves understanding the context in which change must be achieved. Chapter 2 uses critical questions to indicate what principals need to know about their school and its students and community before launching the turnaround process. Attempting school improvement without a solid foundation of local knowledge is unlikely to result in success.

Equipped with a knowledge of the context for change, principals next must be able to reflect on and analyze what they know, a process akin to reaching a diagnosis in medicine. *Turnaround diagnostics*, the subject of chapter 3, leads to the identification of causes of low performance and possible barriers to addressing these causes. Turnaround principals are advised to focus primarily on the causes of low performance that school personnel can control or at least influence.

Leaders of low-performing schools are expected to accomplish quick and dramatic improvements. To do so requires a complex set of advanced planning skills coupled with the sound judgment to know what to focus on and what to defer until a later time. Chapter 4 provides details on the components of a sound School Turnaround Plan. A case is made for moving away from traditional annual plans toward shorter planning cycles and eventually to continuous planning.

School Turnaround Plans consist of goals, objectives, and strategies. There are two major types of strategy. First-order strategies provide the operational foundation needed to support specific academic interventions. Second-order strategies represent these specific interventions. Chapter 5 addresses the first-order strategies that have proven most effective in turning around low-performing schools. They include alignment, instructional improvement, team building, scheduling, professional development, safety and discipline initiatives, family engagement, and faculty building.

Second-order strategies are discussed in chapter 6. In order to make the discussion relevant for leaders of low-performing schools, specific problems faced by these schools are presented along with strategies that have proven helpful in reducing the problems. Among the problems highlighted in the chapter are student absenteeism, poor student work habits, reading difficulties, lack of English language skills, the transition to ninth grade, and high school dropouts.

Chapter 7 focuses on what principals need to accomplish over the summer as they gear up for the turnaround process. Most guidebooks for principals concentrate on completing the plan that will govern the process, but this is only one of a number of critical tasks that must be handled. The chapter discusses negotiations between principals and central office officials, development of the leadership team, filling vacant positions, meeting stakeholders, achieving "quick wins," and planning the kick-off to the new school year. Undertaking these tasks successfully goes a long way to getting the turnaround process off to a good start.

Schools with a track record of low achievement desperately need positive momentum. In order to ensure that progress is made during the first year of the turnaround process, a variety of steps can be taken. To ensure that the School Turnaround Plan is actually implemented, for example, chapter 8 recommends employing project management, a strategy borrowed from businesses. Other important steps include developing organizational routines, making students partners in the turnaround process, and improving school climate.

It is one thing to achieve academic gains in the first year or two of the turn-around process and quite another matter to sustain these gains over the long haul. Chapter 9 looks at some of the keys to sustainability, including adaptive leadership, faculty development, school reculturing, curriculum development beyond English and mathematics, community relations, and trouble-shooting.

One additional key to sustainability involves support from school district leaders. Drawing on studies of various school systems, chapter 10 presents the ways that the district office can reinforce efforts by principals and teachers to raise student achievement and underwrite the school improvement process.

So that's the book in a nutshell. My hope is that it provides principals and school-leaders-to-be with a useful framework for addressing the complexities of leading low-performing schools. I cannot think of a more important or potentially rewarding undertaking.

A FEW WORDS ABOUT THE AUTHOR

My administrative experience with a low-performing school took place in a large, rural, secondary school in upstate New York. My previous teaching experience in Philadelphia had not prepared me for the special challenges of rural poverty and complacency. Then I moved across the country to a faculty position at Stanford University's School of Education. Part of my assignment involved working with a Teacher Corps Project in San Jose, California. During this time Californians passed Proposition 13, a property tax limitation initiative that fostered widespread school decline. I learned that some principals were more effective at limiting the negative impact of reduced funding than other principals.

Over the ensuing four decades I have spent considerable time in low-performing schools, conducting research, consulting with school leaders, and training administrators and teachers. I have written instructional cases on successful school turnarounds and published handbooks on school improvement. I helped develop the University of Virginia's School Turnaround Specialist Program, one of the oldest programs of its kind, and later was involved in designing the Texas Turnaround Leadership Academy and the Florida Turnaround Leaders Program, the largest effort to date by any state to prepare leaders for low-performing schools.

I do not share this information to be boastful, only to indicate that I have immersed myself in the subject matter of this book for a very long time. I have seen successful school turnarounds as well as unfortunate flops. In medicine, grey hair is considered a benefit. I trust that my grey hair indicates a historical perspective on leading low-performing schools that can balance all the hype and misinformation associated with school turnarounds.

Let me close with one lesson about low-performing schools that I have learned over the years. Young people whose best hope for a productive and meaningful life is the school that they attend are not guinea pigs. We must not subject these young people to untested nostrums and possible panaceas on the grounds that "things can't get any worse." Things always can get worse. As educators, we are obliged ethically and professionally to provide young people in low-performing schools with the very best programs and practices that we know. I hope my book serves this purpose for school leaders.

Daniel L. Duke
Charlottesville, Virginia

REFERENCES

Academy for Urban School Leadership. Downloaded from the following website on December 1, 2009: http://www.applitrack.com/ausl/onlineapp/jobpostings/view.asp.

Duke, D. L. 1978. Student behavior, the depersonalization of blame, and the society of victims. *The Journal of Educational Thought*, 12(1), 3–17.

Edmonds, R. 1982. Programs of school improvement: An overview. *Educational Leadership*, 40(3), 4–11.

Stuit, D. A. 2010. *Are Bad Schools Immortal?* Washington, DC: Thomas B. Fordham Institute.

It's All about Leading Change

For leaders of high-performing schools, continuity is critical. Stakeholders are proud of their school and want to maintain its traditions, culture, and academic track record. Leading a low-performing school, on the other hand, is all about change. And not just gradual change. Parents know that their children cannot afford to wait years until improvements are made.

Achieving rapid improvements in a low-performing school is a complex and energy-demanding process. Simplistic prescriptions fail to fit the unique contextual circumstances of individual schools. Still, many of the challenges that must be addressed and overcome in order to turn around low-performing schools are predictable. This chapter begins by noting some of these challenges.

In order to address and overcome challenges, principals need to know a lot about two things—organizational change and change leadership. The second section of this chapter examines what we know about organizational change and how this knowledge applies to turning around low-performing schools. The last section focuses on what is entailed in leading change. This broad overview of challenges, change, and change leadership sets the stage for a closer look at the steps involved in achieving rapid improvements in low-performing schools.

LEADERSHIP CHALLENGES OF SCHOOL TURNAROUND

There is no point in the school turnaround process when challenges to forward progress should not be anticipated by principals. The challenges that can arise at the very outset of improvement efforts, however, are often the most serious, since failure to address them effectively can threaten to slow down or completely derail the entire turnaround process.

Reaching agreement on changes. One early challenge involves securing broad agreement regarding the changes needed in order to raise student achievement. Different stakeholder groups often have strikingly different opinions about what requires fixing. In one study (Duke et al., 2007) of nineteen principals in the Virginia School Turnaround Specialist Program, for example, the conditions judged to be most in need of attention included inadequate personnel, ineffective instruction, lack of data, and ineffective discipline.

Conditions Most Frequently Targeted for Change by Nineteen Turnaround Principals

- Inadequate personnel (18)
- Ineffective instruction (16)
- Lack of data (15)
- Ineffective discipline (13)
- Lack of clear focus/priorities (13)
- Unaligned curriculum content (11)
- Ineffective interventions (11)
- Lack of teamwork (11)
- Low parent involvement (11)
- Inadequate organizational infrastructure (10)

When 320 teachers in schools led by Virginia School Turnaround Specialist Program principals were asked to identify the conditions most in need of attention, their Likert scale ratings revealed a different set of priorities (Duke, Konold, and Salmonowicz, 2011). Table 1.1 indicates that teachers believed

Table 1.1. Conditions Most Frequently Targeted for Change by 320 Teachers in Low-Performing Schools

	Likert Mean
Low parent involvement	1.53
Lack of central office support	1.72
Ineffective interventions	1.81
Lack of community partnerships	1.84
Ineffective discipline	1.86
Inadequate time for reading instruction	1.95
Lack of instructional specialists	2.01

the conditions most requiring improvement were low parent involvement, lack of central office support, ineffective interventions for struggling students, and lack of community partnerships.

The point is not that one group has a more accurate perception of what needs to be changed than another group. The point is that lack of agreement among stakeholders about what needs improvement reduces the likelihood of successful school turnaround. Leaders of low-performing schools, in other words, would be wise to invest time and energy in reaching a reasonable level of agreement about the focus of change efforts. An important part of this process is deciding which problematic conditions school personnel are and are not in a position to change.

Generating a sense of urgency. One might think that getting people invested in rapid change would not be a problem in a low-performing school. Unfortunately, however, if the school has been struggling for a long time, faculty members and even some community residents may not believe that a dramatic turnaround is possible. They can feel like they have tried everything they know without encouraging results. As a result, they settle in to a state of complacency and quiet desperation. Payne (2008) characterizes these schools as demoralized environments because individuals have lost confidence that they can make a difference. Veteran teachers in such environments often regard anyone who tries to make a difference as a threat.

Writing about organizations in general, Kotter (1996) contends that generating a sense of urgency is the first step toward improvement. Leaders who fail to do so rarely achieve desired changes, he argues. No matter how poorly a school is performing, it is likely that many faculty members have developed comfortable routines and found ways to make the most of a sorry situation. Any proposed change therefore may be seen as a cause for apprehension. Instead of embracing change, teachers may be standoffish or even openly resistant.

Generating a sense of urgency is doubly challenging because it must be done without appearing to panic. Veterans on staff may have witnessed too many previous attempts to invoke a sense of crisis in order to justify change. Like the townsfolk who heard one too many cries of "Wolf!" from the shepherd, these individuals are likely to greet crisis claims with skepticism. They must be helped to understand that the status quo is no longer acceptable, but that changes can be undertaken in a deliberate, nonfrantic way.

Inspiring trust. It goes without saying that turning around a low-performing school is a tremendously difficult endeavor. No one can do it alone. The team effort required to achieve quick and dramatic improvements depends, to a great extent, on the ability of principals to inspire trust—trust in their leadership, trust among teachers, and trust between school and community. In an extensive longitudinal study of Chicago elementary schools, trust was found to be a key to school improvement. Researchers concluded that "as trust grew in schools so did improvements in teachers' work orientation, the school's engagement with parents, and the sense of safety and order experienced by students" (Bryk et al., 2010. p. 146).

Trust does not develop without the forming of relationships, and relationships typically take time. Newly appointed turnaround principals, however, may not have a lot of time in which to raise student achievement. That they quickly have to cultivate trust with teachers while simultaneously conveying the message that incompetence and anything less than 100 percent effort will not be tolerated constitutes an additional challenge of turnaround leadership.

Establishing order. One reason why some schools are low performing in the first place is that teachers and administrators have been unable to establish an orderly learning environment. Student achievement suffers when teachers spend lots of time handling discipline problems and students do not feel safe in school. It is not uncommon for turnaround principals to spend their first weeks on the job enforcing rules and promoting safe classrooms and corridors (Duke et al., 2005).

Creating and maintaining an orderly learning environment is no small feat, but the challenge is even greater when order must be established without fostering prison-like conditions. Students are not criminals. They need to feel cared about and cared for. Leadership is required to convince students that the steps being taken to reduce inappropriate and unsafe behavior are not punitive acts, but efforts to foster a culture of cooperation and caring.

Expanding teachers' repertoire. Efforts to help struggling students over the past half century have been characterized by the proliferation of specialists and pull-out programs. Specially trained educators and specially designed programs, of course, have their place in low-performing schools, but they are no substitute for high-quality classroom instruction. Presumably recognition of this fact led advocates of Response to Intervention (RtI) programs to focus Tier 1 efforts on improving the quality of instruction for *all* students.

A major challenge for principals of low-performing schools involves convincing regular education teachers that they are the first line of defense against learning problems. Instead of relying on referrals and push-in specialists, teachers need to expand their repertoire of instructional strategies and interventions and abandon ineffective classroom practices. Unless principals themselves understand what constitutes sound instructional practice and effective interventions, they are unlikely to make much headway in these efforts.

Keeping the focus on low achievers. In a world full of distractions, maintaining focus on anything is a challenge. Leaders of low-performing schools are pulled in many directions. Their primary responsibility, however, is to raise student achievement, especially the achievement of low achievers. While this undertaking is challenging enough, it is made more so for several reasons.

First, student achievement, for better or worse, is equated to scores on state standardized tests. Principals and teachers can lose their jobs if test scores fail to reach designated benchmarks. As important as test scores have become, though, principals cannot allow them to displace children in importance. Regardless of how students perform on tests, they are human beings who deserve care and compassion. School personnel must never lose sight of this fact.

A second challenge concerns the needs of high achievers. While it is understandable that turnaround principals need to focus on low achievers, their efforts must not come at the expense of high achievers. No one's interests are served by neglecting bright students. Hess (2011), among others, argues that too exclusive a focus on reducing the achievement gap can have adverse effects on high achievers. Failure to provide access to challenging academic material and differentiated instruction can result in bright students becoming bored and frustrated.

These half dozen challenges certainly are not the only ones to be faced when leading low-performing schools, but they provide an idea of the range of concerns that principals might have to address. Business-as-usual will not be the order of the day as principals confront challenges such as the ones discussed in this section. Understanding the change process can mean the difference between overcoming these challenges and succumbing to them.

LEADERSHIP CHALLENGES
OF SCHOOL TURNAROUND

- Reaching agreement on the conditions that need to be changed
- Generating a sense of urgency for change without panicking
- Inspiring trust while not tolerating incompetence
- Establishing order while maintaining a caring learning environment
- Expanding teachers' repertoire of instructional strategies and interventions
- Keeping the focus on low achievers without neglecting the needs of high achievers

WHAT DO WE KNOW ABOUT THE CHANGE PROCESS?

Experts on organizational change are fond of saying, "To understand something, try to change it." I'm inclined to think that the opposite statement is just as valid: "To change something, try to understand it." The next chapter goes into detail regarding various ways to learn about the specific circumstances of a low-performing school. This section reviews seven findings about the change process and why turnaround principals should take heed of this knowledge.

A process, not an event. It is tempting to think that a change occurs when something is accomplished—a new policy is approved, a new program is adopted, a new practice is put into operation. Change experts (Hall and Hord, 2001) warn against such thinking. They note that change continues beyond adoption and implementation. In other words, change is an ongoing process in which adjustments continually are made. Sometimes what a particular change evolves into over time bears little resemblance to what was originally intended. Who would have guessed, for example, that zero tolerance discipline policies would have led to so many unforeseen problems for principals?

Principals who understand that change is an ongoing process realize that their responsibility does not end with adoption of a program or approval of a

---

KEYS TO UNDERSTANDING
THE CHANGE PROCESS

1. Change is a process, not an event.
2. Change is a problem of the smallest unit.
3. Change invariably involves loss.
4. Before new ways are learned, unlearning old ways is necessary.
5. Groups can be a powerful means for achieving individual change.
6. Structural change can lead to changes in individual behavior.
7. Change often requires a degree of organizational stability.

---

policy. They must continue to monitor the change in order to ensure that it is properly implemented and that it accomplishes the purpose for which it was intended. They also should be careful about premature celebrations. Nowhere is this admonition more true than with school turnarounds. No sooner do some principals proclaim a reversal of declining student achievement than achievement gains vanish. Turning around a low-performing school does not conclude with the first uptick in test scores.

A problem of the smallest unit. Hall and Hord (2001) also observe that organizational change ultimately depends on individual change. If individual staff members continue doing what they have always done, the likelihood of meaningful organizational change is slight. It is of little value to adopt a new curriculum, for instance, if individual teachers continue to teach the content they always have taught. Students of educational change are rightfully cautious about assuming that new programs and practices actually are in place once classroom doors are shut.

Once again, the message for principals is clear. To ensure that changes take hold, they must continue to monitor and observe staff members. They also need to make certain that individuals have received the training necessary to implement new programs and practices. Assuming that a few staff development workshops are sufficient to alter enduring routines can be a serious mistake. The best chance for individuals to change their practice is for principals to provide continuing training.

The prospect of loss. Low-performing schools can be depressing places characterized by a pervasive sense of frustration and failure. Individuals working in such settings, one might think, would be quick to embrace change. As it turns out, though, even in such adverse circumstances, change can be challenging. One reason is that change frequently involves a sense of loss. Regardless of how bad the situation, people find ways of making it tolerable. What's more, the situation is familiar. The effects of change, on the other hand, are unknown.

Bridges states, "Every transition begins with an ending. We have to let go of the old thing before we can pick up the new one" (2004, p. 11). Leaders of low-performing schools who grasp the significance of this observation are careful to provide staff members with opportunities to discuss what they value about their preturnaround circumstances. They also realize that a clear picture of where the school is headed can reduce some of the anxiety and sense of loss that staff members may associate with the school turnaround process.

The necessity of unlearning. The sixties was a time of widespread educational reform. New curriculums were rolled out in biology, physics, chemistry, anthropology, and mathematics. Despite the millions of dollars spent developing these curriculums, they rarely resulted in changed classroom practice. When he studied the failure of New Math to take hold, Sarason (1971) found that training in New Math was limited to one three-week summer program. No effort was made in the training to have math teachers "unlearn" their traditional math training. They simply were expected to add knowledge of the New Math to concepts and methods they had spent years learning and practicing. It didn't work.

Before adding new knowledge and skills, individuals need to understand why what they already know is no longer sufficient. They need examples to illustrate the advantages of what they are being asked to learn. In some cases they need to practice their old methods in tandem with the new methods in order to see the latter's benefits. Principals must understand that the goal of training has less to do with adding new knowledge to old than with replacing old knowledge with new. Needless to say, the latter process requires more time than the former.

The power of groups. While it is true that low-performing schools are unlikely to change unless the individuals working in them change, it is also the case that groups can be powerful drivers of individual change (Katz and Kahn, 1978). When group members share the perception that change is needed, for example, the likelihood of change is greatly increased. The opposite also is true. Group resistance can be a major impediment to reform.

Educators identify with various school-based groups. Grade-level groups, teaching teams, academic departments, and Professional Learning Communities are some of the groups that can exert influence on the beliefs and behavior of teachers. Principals who understand the potential power of groups facilitate the school turnaround process by working with and through school-based groups. When, however, groups function as potent sources of resistance to change, breaking up groups may be the first order of business.

Structural change as an impetus. Another key to individual change is structural change (Bolman and Deal, 1997). Schools consist of various structural arrangements, including grade-levels, departments, teams, schedules, and roles. Additional structures are intended to ensure high-quality performance. These include policies, rules, personnel and program evaluation, supervision, incentives, and sanctions. Making adjustments to structures can have an effect on both individual and group performance.

Consider collaborative planning and data-driven decision making, two widely recognized characteristics of successful school turnarounds. Teachers are much more likely to embrace these important functions if time to meet together is built into the school's weekly schedule. Relying on teachers to find time before or after school to plan and analyze data often proves to be problematic.

Another structural change that has attracted the attention of policy makers involves linking teacher evaluations to student achievement. While this measure has raised anxiety and created new challenges for principals, it is still unclear whether or not there are benefits for students. Structural adjustments that have been shown to contribute to improved teaching and learning include extended learning time, collaborative teaching, and classroom walkthroughs.

The need for stability. It sounds like an oxymoron, but change experts have come to the conclusion that successful change depends on a certain degree of stability (Kanter, 1988). When everything seems to be changing at once, people become overwhelmed and disoriented. Under such circumstances, they may resist all change efforts, even those that are well-intentioned and carefully planned. Some degree of continuity therefore may be necessary before people are willing to undertake a change initiative.

Principals who understand the need for stability and continuity are careful to focus on a few changes at a time. Doing so assures people that their work environment will remain reasonably familiar while selected reforms are being made. An added benefit of focused change is the increased likelihood of successful implementation. It is far easier for school leaders to monitor and manage a small number of changes than a wholesale revolution.

Principles of organizational change such as the seven discussed in this section provide turnaround principals with important guidance as they undertake the process of school improvement. They are only part of the story, however. Principals also need to know about what it takes to lead a low-performing school.

WHAT DO WE KNOW ABOUT CHANGE LEADERSHIP?

If every principal were up to the challenges of school turnaround, there would not be thousands of chronically low-performing schools. We already know that an understanding of the change process is an invaluable asset for turnaround principals. What are some other essentials for leading low-performing schools?

Desire to make a difference. First and foremost, a principal must want to make a difference. Plenty of individuals want to lead, but the desire to make a difference goes beyond wanting to lead. It involves wanting to lead for a purpose—a purpose greater than one's own career ambitions and ego needs.

The origins of desire can vary greatly. Some individuals may have grown up poor and attended low-performing schools. They appreciate what it takes to escape the pull of poverty and ineffective schooling, and they want to make sure that children of modest means receive a good education. Other individuals may have been raised in relatively well-to-do homes, but they are committed to levelling the playing field as much as they can by ensuring that less fortunate youngsters receive a high-quality education. Still others may regard leading low-performing schools as a spiritual calling and a moral obligation.

Whatever the source of their commitment, difference makers begin by asking themselves the first question of leadership—"*What do I need to do?*" They do not begin by wondering what changes others need to make. If you cannot see yourself at the epicenter of change, you're probably not the right person for initiating school turnaround.

Ability to provide direction. Ambiguity and uncertainty are endemic to schools, especially low-performing schools. Educators frequently feel as if they are being pulled and pushed in many directions. Is schooling supposed to be about passing tests or is there more to it than that? Are all students supposed to receive the same education? How should scarce resources be allocated? Opinions vary widely on these and other issues. Providing stakeholders with a clear sense of direction is not easy, but it is fundamental to turnaround leadership.

Direction refers to long-term goals. Direction, in and of itself, is not a panacea, however. Some long-term goals are more likely to inspire commitment and cooperation than others. The art of leadership involves determining a direction that best serves the needs of stakeholders and then articulating it in ways that cause them to embrace the direction.

Discipline to focus. While direction is necessary, it is not sufficient for launching the turnaround process. Direction without focus is unlikely to produce desired results. There are so many things that need to be done in a low-performing school that trying to tackle them all at the same time is a recipe for failure. But focus requires discipline. Principals must be able to decide what to focus on first and then maintain that focus despite the never-ending distractions that characterize contemporary school leadership. Direction is the domain of the designer. Focus is the architect's turf.

Just as not all directions are well suited to a particular low-performing school, so some foci are better than others. Turnaround principals must draw on school data and a knowledge of their faculty and community in order to judge what to focus on first. Choosing a focus with little likelihood of success or selecting too many objectives to focus on at one time can stall the turnaround process before it ever gets off the ground.

Creativity to plan. Schools are not turned around because of good intentions alone. Direction and focus must be embodied in a plan that provides stakeholders with the guidance necessary to improve achievement. An effective School Turnaround Plan, however, requires considerable creativity. A principal must bring together the right combination of people to develop the plan, help them to make sense of the data on which the plan is based, choose sound strategies for addressing focal concerns, and secure the resources needed to execute the plan. The planning process resembles putting together the pieces to a complex puzzle.

Turnaround principals know that the puzzle pieces available to them do not always fit. That's where creativity is required. How can existing personnel be reassigned in order to increase effectiveness? What new sources of data can be tapped? Can current strategies that are not working be tweaked in order to improve results or must they be replaced? Can additional funding and assistance be secured? Successful turnaround principals never stop searching for new and better ways to meet the needs of their students.

Flexibility to adjust. A sound School Turnaround Plan is essential, but it is unrealistic to think that every component of such a plan will work perfectly. Despite careful analysis of data and creative thinking, some reforms may not work very well. Then there are the challenges that planners have no way of anticipating. School boundaries that are redrawn. Staff turnover. Unforeseen policy changes from state and federal policy makers.

A lot is heard about implementation fidelity and staying the course. While it is true that improvement strategies should be given a fair chance to succeed, it is also the case that some strategies may prove to be poorly suited to a school's needs. Under such circumstances, turnaround principals must be prepared to make appropriate adjustments to their School Turnaround Plan. Sticking with a course of action or changing course is rarely an easy decision to make, but it is the kind of judgment call that distinguishes successful turnaround principals from unsuccessful turnaround principals.

Patience to persist. Turning around a low-performing school can resemble riding a roller coaster. There are high points and low points on the journey to school improvement. The low points have been characterized by terms like *implementation dip* and *reform fatigue.* When all the hard work and dedication to helping struggling students fails to produce the desired outcomes, staff members understandably become disappointed. At such points in the turnaround process, leadership is most critical.

Knowing that low points in the turnaround process are predictable actually can be an advantage. Only those with illusions in the first place become disillusioned. Successful turnaround principals are prepared to persist in the

KEYS TO CHANGE LEADERSHIP

- Desire to make a difference
- Ability to provide direction
- Discipline to focus
- Creativity to plan
- Flexibility to adjust
- Patience to persist

face of disappointment. They are constantly on the lookout for evidence of improvement, no matter how small. One student's improved attendance. Another student's unexpected success on an interim test. Small victories accumulate and help offset the impact of lower-than-expected outcomes on high-stakes tests and other performance indicators.

You will notice that the keys to change leadership are not just a matter of skill. They also involve character and temperament. As you read the rest of this book, you will see how turnaround principals put these keys to change leadership into action. Understanding what principals do to improve low-performing schools may not ensure your own success as a turnaround principal, but it should provide a solid basis for determining whether you are up to the challenge.

REFERENCES

Bolman, L. G. and Deal, T. E. 1997. *Reframing Organizations*, 2nd ed. San Francisco: Jossey-Bass.

Bridges, W. 2004. *Transitions*. Cambridge, MA: DaCapo.

Bryk, A. S.; Sebring, P. B.; Allensworth, E.; Luppescu, S.; and Easton, J. Q. 2010. *Organizing Schools for Improvement*. Chicago: University of Chicago Press.

Duke, D. L.; Konold, T.; and Salmonowicz, M. 2011. Teacher perceptions of what needs to be changed in low-performing schools. *ERS Spectrum*, 29(1), 1–15.

Duke, D. L.; Tucker, P. D.; Belcher, M.; Crews, D.; Harrison-Coleman, J.; Higgins, J.; Lanphear, L.; Marshall, M.; Reasor, H.; Richardson, S.; Rose, M.; Salmonowicz, M. J.; Scott, W.; Taylor, R.; Thomas, C.; and West, J. 2005. *Lift-Off: Launching the School Turnaround Process in Ten Virginia Schools.* Charlottesville, VA: Darden-Curry Partnership for Leaders in Education, University of Virginia.

Duke, D. L.; Tucker, P. D.; Salmonowicz, M. J.; and Levy, M. 2007. How comparable are the perceived challenges facing principals of low-performing schools? *International Studies in Educational Administration*, 35(1), 3–21.

Hall, G. E. and Hord, S. M. 2001. *Implementing Change*. Boston: Allyn & Bacon.

Hess, F. M. 2011. Our achievement gap mania. *National Affairs*, (9), 113–129. Downloaded from: http://www.nationalaffairs.com/publications/detail/our-achievement-gap-mania.

Kanter, R. M. 1988. When a thousand flowers bloom: structural, collective, and social conditions for innovation in organization. In B. M. Staw and L. L. Cummings (eds.), *Research in Organizational Behavior*, Vol. 10. Greenwich, CT: JAI Press, 169–211.

Katz, D. and Kahn, R. L. 1978. *The Social Psychology of Organizations*, 2nd ed. New York: Wiley.

Kotter, J. P. 1996. *Leading Change*. Boston: Harvard Business School Press.

Payne, C. M. 2008. *So Much Reform, So Little Change*. Cambridge, MA: Harvard Education Press.

Sarason, S. B. 1971. *The Culture of the School and the Problem of Change*. Boston: Allyn & Bacon.

2

Launching the
Turnaround Process

If school improvement is an ongoing process and not a one-time event, where does the process begin?

Consider what the initial stages of school turnaround might look like from a principal's perspective. It is late spring or early summer. You have been appointed principal of a low-performing school. State test scores for your school have just been received. Designated benchmarks once again have not been met. Your school will continue in "improvement" status, meaning it will be subject to intense scrutiny by district and state officials.

The superintendent has made it clear that student achievement needs to be raised and raised quickly. Parents are concerned, and the School Board is considering closing the school if gains cannot be made.

You instinctively know that many changes are needed, but experience has taught you that everything cannot be changed at once. You face the first of what will be a succession of judgment calls. What should be the first focus of action? You realize that how you choose to begin the turnaround process will go a long way toward determining whether or not it succeeds.

PLANNING TO PLAN

Most principals of low-performing schools are required to develop a School Turnaround Plan that specifies student achievement goals, objectives associated with the goals, and strategies for achieving the objectives. Typically much of the work on this plan is accomplished during the summer when school is not in session. This can be both an advantage and a disadvantage. Summer planning benefits from the fact that principals have more free time to analyze data and develop a plan. The disadvantage is that there is less available data in the summer. Classes are not in session, teachers are on vacation, and students are unavailable for input.

While the discussion in this chapter assumes that work on the School Turnaround Plan commences in the summer, it should be noted that starting the planning process in the spring while school is still in session can be very beneficial.[1] Even though scores on state tests may not yet be available, valuable input from teachers and students can be compiled. This input will help school administrators make sense of test data when it eventually is received.

———

Turnaround Tip: Begin to plan the turnaround process in the spring while school is still in session.

———

Before the actual development of a School Turnaround Plan begins, data will need to be gathered. The better the data, the better the plan. Planning to plan involves deciding what data will be collected and analyzed. Those who eventually will be engaged in determining goals, objectives, and strategies will depend on this data to create a plan that addresses high priority needs.

One difference between successful and unsuccessful School Turnaround Plans is the quality of the data on which they are based. The fact is that not all data is of equal value. Some principals, for example, rely too heavily on hearsay and advice from individuals pushing particular agendas. They do not make a sufficient effort to gather a balanced set of opinions. Other principals focus exclusively on state testing data, failing to recognize the value of other sources of student achievement data.

Stressing the importance of a range of data is not to say, however, that school turnaround planning is an exact science. It is not as if there is one universally agreed upon approach to every academic problem. Principals must factor in past performance, community expectations, school history, staff capabilities, available resources, and other variables. Developing a School

Turnaround Plan, in the final analysis, is a matter of judgment. Many judgments, to be more accurate.

Judgments involve difficult choices between two or more options (Mowen, 1993). Furthermore, the information available to the person or persons making the judgment can be ambiguous. There is no clear-cut path to take. Arriving at sound judgments often requires turnaround principals to take into account what is legal or mandated, what is feasible, what is ethical, and what has been shown to be effective. When such considerations are aligned, judgments may be relatively straightforward, but when they conflict, principals are likely to experience significant stress. The broader the range of available information, the better the odds that a sound judgment will be made.

In one study of the judgments made by fourteen turnaround principals, I identified different aspects of the turnaround process that called for tough judgments (Duke, 2012). Setting priorities, for example, required principals to make trade-offs. One elementary principal knew that reading levels were low at all grades, but he decided to focus on the intermediate grades first, leaving the primary grades for the following year. He reasoned that it was more important to prepare fourth and fifth graders for middle school than to zero in on students in the lower grades. There would be time later to address reading problems in the lower grades.

Another area for judgments involved setting measurable targets for School Turnaround Plans. Setting targets too high can lead to disappointment and public criticism. Setting targets too low can cause teachers to approach the turnaround process too casually. Principals had to spend time analyzing past scores on state tests in order to determine achievement targets that were attainable.

Some of the most challenging judgments concerned identifying the probable causes of low achievement. Were low scores in mathematics the result of a mismatch between the current math program and student needs, or were teachers not teaching the math program as it was designed to be taught? Were teachers failing to provide struggling students with adequate assistance in math, or were struggling students failing to take advantage of opportunities for help? Often the answers to questions like these are complicated, making judgments about what action to take even more challenging.

Not surprisingly, some of the most difficult judgments involved personnel. Was a particular teacher, for example, likely to improve instructionally with focused professional development and support, or would the interests of students be better served by replacing the teacher with a more skilled individual? In the case of the latter judgment, what is the likelihood of finding a more skilled teacher?

The judgments involved in planning school turnarounds are, by nature, guesswork. Still, there is a vast difference between guesswork based on a solid foundation of data and guesswork grounded in uninformed speculation. The first step in planning to plan, therefore, should be determining what data is needed for planning purposes.

A THEORY OF ACTION FOR ACHIEVING SCHOOL TURNAROUND

A *theory of action* is a set of assertions regarding what is required to accomplish a challenging goal. The goal in this case is to reverse a pattern of low or declining student achievement and start a school moving in a positive direction. The following assertions are based on the experiences of successful turnaround principals.

1. *Awareness.* Low-performing schools frequently are characterized by similar problems, but they also can have unique problems associated with their communities, mix of students, and school cultures. Educators cannot correct problems of which they are unaware. Leading a school turnaround therefore begins with generating widespread awareness of the academic problems that must be corrected in order to raise student achievement.

It is equally important to note areas of academic performance where students are performing relatively well. Dwelling on negative data and failing to acknowledge positive outcomes can undermine school turnaround efforts and discourage educators. Later in this chapter, various sources of data on academic performance will be identified.

2. *Causal understanding.* Awareness of academic problems is necessary, but insufficient by itself, to produce successful school turnarounds. It is also important to understand the causes of academic problems. Such understanding results from examining additional data sources in order to learn how academic problems have been and are being addressed. The root causes of some academic problems, of course, are external to the school. Poverty and parenting are two of the most widely discussed of these external causes. Since educators can do relatively little to alter external causes, the focus of causal understanding should be the *school-based causes of academic problems* that

are susceptible to corrective action. These causes include ineffective instruction, curriculum misalignment, inadequate performance feedback, and lack of assistance for struggling students.

The process of developing causal understanding—referred to in this book as *turnaround diagnostics*—is discussed in chapter 3. It is important to note that turnaround diagnostics differs from the process by which teachers and specialists diagnose a particular student's learning issues. Turnaround diagnostics requires (1) the identification of academic problems that characterize significant groups of students, and (2) the subsequent determination of school-based causes of these problems.

3. *Continuous planning.* Awareness of academic problems and their likely school-based causes provide the foundation for school turnaround planning. Such planning, however, should not be regarded simply as the production of a detailed plan once a year. While a written plan certainly can be a useful tool, especially when it is coupled with project management (to be explained later), planning needs to be ongoing in order to be effective.

An important reason for continuous planning is the fact that useful planning data is not always available at a given point in time. Planning that takes place over the summer, for instance, cannot take advantage of observational data on new faculty members hired during summer break. Thorough analyses of student performance for each section of state standardized tests may be unavailable until the end of the summer.

It is best to think of planning as a process that pervades the entire school. Emphasis in this book is placed on school-wide turnaround planning, which is a focal point of leadership for low-performing schools; but if planning only takes place at the top, the likelihood of school improvement is slight. Grade-level and departmental planning are critical for such functions as curriculum alignment, common assessment, and professional development. Planning also is essential to ensure that the needs of struggling students are addressed systematically.

4. *Execution.* Planning, of course, is of little value unless plans are executed. It is anything but a foregone conclusion that a developed plan is an implemented plan. The folklore of schooling acknowledges that School Turnaround Plans frequently gather dust in the principal's office. Often developed over the summer, plans gradually recede into the background as the school year proceeds.

A key component of planning is determining the school's capacity to execute the plan (Bossidy and Charan, 2009). Execution requires competence, commitment, and communications. School Turnaround Plans consist of various objectives and strategies involving many or all staff members. Ultimately it is the principal's responsibility to see that staff members have the skills and knowledge to implement the plan as well as the willingness to do so. Successful execution also depends on frequent feedback regarding how well implementation is going.

5. *Adjustment.* This point was made in the previous chapter: leading school turnaround requires flexibility. No plan, however carefully developed and well executed, is guaranteed to work. Football coaches carefully plan how each game will be played, but they still have to make adjustments in their game plan as the game unfolds. So, too, with School Turnaround Plans. Continuous planning facilitates adjustment by providing regular opportunities to monitor progress on goals and objectives and determine when strategies are not working well.

Businesses often plan on a quarterly (90-day) basis. School planning, until recently, tended to be done exclusively on a yearly basis. When planning is an annual process, staff members are more likely to wait until the end of the school year before assessing how well strategies have been working. Sometimes, of course, it is important to give strategies a fair chance to succeed, but in other cases, waiting until June to scrap a strategy can cost valuable time and place affected students at a disadvantage for the next school year. Plans that are reassessed periodically can be modified in time to prevent these losses.

THEORY OF ACTION FOR
ACHIEVING SCHOOL TURNAROUND

1. Awareness
2. Causal understanding
3. Continuous planning
4. Execution
5. Adjustment

DATA GATHERING CONSIDERATIONS

Educators are constantly gathering data and making causal inferences. They observe a student falling asleep in class and blame it on boredom. They receive a poorly done assignment and attribute it to lack of motivation? These speculations, however, are not always accurate. When I was a new assistant principal in a rural secondary school and I received reports from several teachers that students were falling asleep in their late morning classes, my first thought was that the students were using drugs. My previous experience had been in an urban high school where drug use was prevalent. What I did not realize was that many students in my new school awoke at 4:00 a.m. to milk cows and perform other farm chores. By late morning their energy levels were low and they needed food to recharge their batteries.

To guard against errors in data gathering and analysis like the one I made, principals should consider the following tips when compiling data on student achievement and related topics.

First, it is generally unwise to rely on a single source of data. Too often, for example, important judgments about student achievement are based solely on the scores from a single standardized test. There can be many reasons why students do not perform well on a particular test. Perhaps the test did not align well with what students were taught. Or the test was culturally biased. Maybe students were preoccupied with recent events at their school or at home. The only sure way to determine whether or not a test score accurately reflects student learning is to look at related indicators of achievement such as grades, work samples, and performance on interim or benchmark tests.

—⊗⊗⊗—

Turnaround Tip: Whenever possible, draw on multiple sources of data before drawing conclusions about student achievement.

—⊗⊗⊗—

A second consideration involves the appropriate unit of data analysis for the question or questions being investigated. The following are four frequently used units:

1. grade level,
2. subject or course,
3. teacher, and
4. student cohort.

Each unit of data analysis is suited to a somewhat different purpose. Compiling student achievement data by grade level, for instance, provides insight into how all the students (and teachers) at a certain grade level are performing in a given school year. Alternatively, the focus of analysis may be student achievement in a particular subject area such as Algebra 1. Under certain circumstances, it also may be important to determine how one teacher's students are performing in comparison to another teacher's students. A fourth option involves tracking the performance of one or more cohorts of students over time. Tracking the performance of a student cohort over several years, for example, is a better way to determine the cumulative effects of inadequate instruction and poor curriculum articulation than focusing on performance at one grade level in a particular year.

A fifth option involves aggregating achievement data for all students in a school for a given year. Using the entire school as the unit of data analysis may be useful for state education officials who want to grade and compare schools, but such aggregated data is of little use to principals needing to focus turnaround efforts on a few high priority goals.

Turnaround Tip: Consider alternative units of data analysis when compiling data on student achievement.

When compiling and analyzing student achievement data in order to develop School Turnaround Plans, it is best to focus initially on trends and central tendencies in the data rather than outliers and exceptions. Trends across time periods serve as a useful basis for investigating the school-based causes of decline (and progress) in student achievement. Comparing trends in the data for different subgroups also can lead to important diagnostic questions. Individual outliers and exceptions should not be ignored, of course, but they are better addressed by intervention teams *after* schoolwide planning has been undertaken.

Turnaround Tip: The focus of data gathering and analysis for schoolwide planning should be trends in the data rather than exceptions.

A third consideration concerns the amount of data to be collected and analyzed at any point in time. When planners are inundated in data, they may not be able to focus their analysis in productive ways (Duke, Carr, and Sterrett, 2013). Data gathering and analysis should be regarded as iterative processes. Planners begin with a set of data—say state test results in mathematics for the last five years. Examining this data generates questions and tentative explanations that, in turn, call for additional data. Making data gathering and analysis a selective endeavor guided by the analysis of previously examined data increases the efficiency and effectiveness of school turnaround planning.

Turnaround Tip: Instead of gathering and analyzing all student achievement data at one time, undertake data collection and analysis in manageable increments.

Academic Achievement Data

The reason that some schools need to be turned around is that large numbers of their students are not demonstrating sufficient academic achievement to enable them to access higher education or secure good jobs after graduation. Some of these students will not even be able to graduate from high school. So, it is not surprising that the data that first needs to be compiled and analyzed is student academic achievement data. Raising academic achievement must be the primary goal of School Turnaround Plans, and planners need to understand where students stand academically before they can choose specific targets for improvement.

Because the bases for federal, state, and district accountability systems are state standardized testing programs for elementary and secondary students, turnaround principals typically begin by reviewing the most recent set of state test results. While states vary somewhat in what and when they test, most states test for reading/language arts and mathematics proficiency in grades 3 through 8. States also may test in science and social studies in these grades. High school students are tested in English/language arts and mathematics as well. Many states additionally have introduced end-of-course tests in selected high school subjects such as Algebra 1 and U.S. History.

State standardized tests are based on state curriculum standards. Official reports of state testing frequently include breakdowns of results by standard, thereby providing principals with important information regarding areas of the curriculum where students are achieving relatively well and relatively poorly. Principals also can use these reports to determine how various student subgroups are performing relative to other subgroups and relative to peers from other schools in the state. Results from previous years' testing reports can be consulted to determine whether student academic achievement is improving, declining, or holding steady.

While clearly of primary importance, the results of state standardized tests are only one of many sources of valuable data regarding academic achievement. Consider the list of additional data sources in the box below.

Imagine that you are the principal of a chronically low-performing school. You appoint a team of key staff members to join you in examining a variety of student academic achievement data. Before diving into the data, you ask

STUDENT ACHIEVEMENT DATA SOURCES

- Diagnostic tests in reading and mathematics
- Interim and benchmark tests aligned to state standards
- Teacher-made tests and quizzes
- Class assignments and projects
- Student course selections
- Student responses to teacher questions
- Student questions during class
- Homework
- Grades
- Observations of students at work
- External tests (PSAT, SAT, ACT, Advanced Placement, International Baccalaureate, etc.)

each team member to write down some questions that they would like to have answered regarding student achievement. Unless they are new to the school, these individuals already should have some questions in mind. Possible questions might include the following:

Sample Questions

- What is the trend in student achievement in reading/language arts and mathematics over the past five years?
- How are students achieving when looked at on a cohort-by-cohort basis?
- How are students achieving when one cohort is tracked over several years?
- In what subjects are students doing relatively well/poorly?
- How are particular student subgroups achieving relative to other subgroups ?
- What do achievement results look like when scores of students who missed more than fifteen days of school are set aside?
- What do achievement results look like when scores of students who transferred to the school in the current year are set aside?
- In what subjects is the least and greatest progress being made in closing achievement gaps between student subgroups ?
- Do student grades reflect their performance on state standardized tests?
- Is the percentage of students achieving high scores (top quartile) on state tests increasing or decreasing?
- Do scores on interim/benchmark tests accurately predict scores on annual state tests?
- What percentage of students are enrolled in honors or Advanced Placement courses?
- What percentage of students in honors or Advanced Placement courses are getting high grades?

Asking team members to write questions *before* investigating achievement data provides principals with an idea of what is and is not on their minds. If a large number of questions is generated by the group, it may be necessary to choose a subset of questions to focus on in order to get started. Team members may discover, once they being reviewing achievement data, that they do not have the data they need to answer certain questions. Ways to obtain the necessary data should be explored at this point. If it is summer, the team may have to wait until the school year begins to gather some of the needed data.

In my experience, data review teams rarely suggest comparing their school's performance with other schools. Collecting achievement data from schools with similar demographics and higher levels of student achievement, however, can serve as an important wake-up call for staff members who believe that nothing more can be done to raise the achievement of their students.

The first objective of the data review team is to develop statements to answer each of the questions they have chosen to focus on. If, for example, a question concerns a subject in which students performed better last year than this year, the data-based statement might read as follows:

Of students taking the end-of-course test in Algebra 1 last year, 54 percent got a passing score as compared to 42 percent of students taking the end-of-course test in Algebra 1 this year.

Statements such as this one then become the basis for the next step in turn-around planning. Why did students do better in Algebra 1 last year than this year? Was there a change in Algebra 1 teachers? Did this year's students have greater problems with middle school mathematics than last year's students? Was there a change in the state's end-of-course test? Or in the Algebra 1 text-book? Did this year's Algebra 1 students miss more days of school than last year's students? The possible reasons performances differ are numerous. The diagnostic process to pinpoint probable explanations is discussed in chapter 3. Before moving on, however, it is important to consider other sources of student data that can be useful when the causes of low academic achievement are explored later on.

Attendance, Behavior, and Beliefs

Besides data on student achievement, schools routinely collect data on student attendance and behavior. Some schools also survey students periodically to learn how they think and feel about their educational experiences. These data sources offer insights into the reasons why some students struggle while other students do relatively well in their schoolwork.

Attendance. Attendance data covers several categories of information, including absenteeism from school, absenteeism from class, absenteeism from tutorials and assistance programs, and tardiness. These data sources can help to explain academic problems for obvious reasons: if students are not in school or they miss particular classes and help sessions, they are less likely to learn what they are expected to learn. When large percentages of students miss certain classes, their absence also may be an indication of relational issues between students and teachers.

Discipline. Data related to discipline problems in and out of class also should be part of any planning for school turnaround. When classrooms are disorderly and corridors are unsafe, learning is affected. Usually some classes are less orderly than others, an indication that some teachers may have difficulty with classroom management. Serious discipline problems lead to suspensions and even expulsions, thereby depriving certain students of the opportunity to learn. Students misbehave and break class and school rules for various reasons. Some of these reasons include academic difficulties, frustration, lack of teacher attention, and even boredom.

Academic behaviors. In recent years education scholars have taken great interest in so-called "noncognitive" factors affecting the academic success of students (Tough, 2012). The point they make is that doing well in school involves more than the accumulation of knowledge and technical skills. Among the noncognitive factors identified by researchers at the Consortium for Chicago School Research (Farrington et al., 2012) is academic behavior. Five academic behaviors were found to be associated with school success: going to class, doing homework, organizing material, participating in class, and studying.

That these academic behaviors have been found to play an important role in student achievement, of course, comes as no surprise to veteran educators. The point of bringing up the subject here is to suggest that it may be useful to gather data concerning such matters as homework completion, how much time students spend studying for tests, whether students study for tests in groups or alone, and which students rarely participate in class. Some data on academic behaviors can be observed in school, while other data is best collected directly from students and parents.

Beliefs about learning. Another dimension of noncognitive factors affecting achievement concerns students' beliefs and feelings about learning. Dweck (2006), for instance, has explored the differences in learning success between individuals with a growth mindset and those with a fixed mindset. The latter limit their learning by avoiding situations where they might appear to know little. Those with growth mindsets, on the other hand, are willing to risk appearing like a novice because they care more about gaining skill and knowledge.

The researchers at the Consortium for Chicago School Research (Farrington et al., 2012) draw on Dweck's work in an effort to illustrate what is involved in having an *academic mindset*. Students with an academic mindset feel that they belong in an academic environment. They believe that effort pays off and leads to growth in competence. They also value learning and doing well in school.

Once again, the point is that educators planning to turn around low-performing schools can benefit by finding out how students feel about learning. Sometimes student surveys can provide this information, but individual interviews and student focus groups probably are a more reliable source of beliefs and feelings about school work.

SUMMING UP LOW PERFORMANCE

Data gathering on student achievement and related topics is likely to reveal a predictable pattern of problems. Significant numbers of students probably are reading well below grade level and struggling with academic vocabulary and comprehension. Achievement in mathematics, regardless of the grade level, also is likely.

Low-performing schools typically are characterized by relatively high rates of absenteeism and misconduct. Students frequently transfer into and out of these schools, challenging teachers to try to catch up new arrivals even as they bid goodbye to students they have worked hard to help. Safety concerns can be so great in many low-performing schools that they take precedence over academic matters.

As for academic behaviors and beliefs about learning, low-performing schools tend to be populated by large numbers of students who miss classes even when they are in school, participate little in class, and fail to complete assignments. It is hard to imagine that these students feel that they really belong in an academic environment or that hard work will pay off in the end.

So, if low-performing schools are likely to share so many similar characteristics, why should turnaround principals bother collecting data?

Despite the seeming similarities, no two low-performing schools are exactly alike. Struggling students in one school may be further behind on some state standards or in certain subjects than their counterparts across town.

Even if students in two schools are found to have almost identical patterns of low achievement, the reasons for low achievement can vary in significant ways. No two schools have exactly the same mix of students. The competence and commitment of faculty members vary across schools, as does the level of parent and community support. Turnaround principals must never assume that all low-performing schools are basically the same. All of which is to say that data gathering and analysis is always a sound way to launch the turnaround process.

Turnaround Tip: Never assume that all low-performing schools are alike.

NOTE

1. If a turnaround principal is appointed during the summer, beginning to plan in the spring, of course, will not be possible.

REFERENCES

Bossidy, L. and Charan, R. 2009. *Execution.* New York: Crown Business.

Duke, D. L. 2012. The judgment of principals. In B. G. Barnett, A. R. Shoho, and A. T. Cypres (eds.). *The Changing Nature of Instructional Leadership in the 21st Century.* Charlotte, N. C.: Information Age Publishing, 13–32.

Duke, D. L.; Carr, M.; and Sterrett, W. 2013. *The School Improvement Planning Handbook.* Lanham, MD: Rowman & Littlefield.

Dweck, C. S. 2006. *Mindset.* New York: Ballantine Books.

Farrington, C. A.; Roderick, M.; Allensworth, E.; Nagaoka, J.; Keyes, T. S.; Johnson, D. W.; and Beechum, N. O. 2012. *Teaching Adolescents to Become Learners.* Chicago: Consortium for Chicago School Research, University of Chicago.

Mowen, J. C. 1993. *Judgment Calls.* New York: Simon & Schuster.

Tough, P. 2012. *How Children Succeed.* Boston: Houghton Mifflin Harcourt.

Diagnosing the Causes of Low Performance

Whenever test results for schools are announced, it seems that everyone has an explanation for why some schools have lower scores than other schools. The redesigned tests must have placed students from poor neighborhoods at a disadvantage. Teacher turnover was very high in low-performing schools. The number of English language learners increased at schools with low pass rates in reading. These explanations, or "causal stories" as Stone (1989) prefers, can play a critical role in the turnaround process.

Consider a hypothetical situation. Test results are reported for two high schools in adjoining school districts. One high school receives significantly higher scores than the other. Individuals and groups flood the local newspaper with opinion pieces concerning the low-performing school. One argument focuses on the lower pay scale for teachers. The implication is that the low-performing school is not attracting and keeping as talented a group of teachers as the high-performing school.

Another opinion piece blames the principal. She is accused of lacking skill as an instructional leader. A letter to the editor from the local teachers association blames parents for not being more involved in their children's education. An educational researcher from a nearby university contends that the low-performing high school assigns too many students to nonrigorous "basic" courses instead of academically challenging honors and Advanced Placement courses.

Causal stories are important because gaining acceptance for a particular causal story determines, to a great extent, what will be done to correct low performance. Should district officials for the low-performing high school in the preceding example raise teacher salaries to attract more talented teachers? Or should the principal be replaced? Or should a campaign be mounted to increase parental involvement? Or should more students be assigned to honors and Advanced Placement courses?

Each explanation leads to a different solution, and each solution is characterized by different costs and possible consequences. What's more, each of the causal stories may be only partially correct. Just as the consequences of an incorrect or partially correct diagnosis by a physician can be disastrous, so too with acceptance of the wrong causal story for low school performance.

Payne (2008), in fact, contends that the failure of school leaders to diagnose accurately the causes of student achievement problems is itself a major contributor to low performance. As he puts it, "people in leadership positions do not have a systemic understanding of the causes of failure, in part because the same dysfunctional social arrangements that do so much to cause failure also do a great deal to obscure its origins" (p. 5).

The present chapter looks closely at the data that may be needed in order to arrive at accurate diagnoses of student achievement problems. Several ways to collect and analyze the data also are discussed.

AN ABUNDANCE OF CAUSES

Diagnosing the causes of low achievement would be a fruitless and frustrating endeavor if educators were unable to impact any of the causes. Before reviewing various causes, it may be helpful for you to consider your own beliefs regarding the causes that educators are most and least likely to impact. The following pages contain a "Checklist of Possible Causes of Low Student Achievement," an instrument that I developed for the Florida Turnaround Leaders Program (FTLP). The FTLP is one of the most ambitious efforts to date to prepare school turnaround leaders. The checklist contains a variety of causes of low achievement that have been identified by educators and researchers. Review the list and see how many of the causes you believe can be highly impacted by educators.[1]

The literature concerning low student achievement addresses two general concerns: (1) achievement gaps between different groups of students (Mur-

Table 3.1. Checklist of Possible Causes of Low Student Achievement

Listed below are various causes of low student achievement that have been identified in the research literature. For each cause, place a check in the column that you believe is most appropriate.

Cause of Low Student Achievement	The Degree to Which Educators Can Impact This Cause			
	No Impact	Low Impact	Moderate Impact	High Impact*
Peer pressure not to do well in school				
Inadequate parent supervision				
Ineffective instruction				
Lack of student motivation to succeed in school				
Low expectations on the part of school staff				
Poverty				
Disorderly classrooms				
Inadequate monitoring of student progress				
Discriminatory practices by school personnel				
High student mobility				
Ineffective interventions for struggling students				
High teacher-student ratio				
Lack of highly qualified teachers				
Inadequately aligned curriculum				
School schedule that lacks time for planning				
Inadequate focus on raising achievement by school leaders				
Inadequate resources				
Negative, uncaring school culture				
Lack of access to learning opportunities outside of school				
Student absenteeism				
Inadequate English language skills				
Lack of parent involvement in children's schooling				
Unsafe school environment				
Loss of learning over summer months				
"Dumbed down" courses				
Inadequate teacher training				
Ineffective principals				
Schools that are too large				
Low teacher efficacy/confidence				

*High Impact—sufficient to eliminate or significantly reduce the cause phy, 2010) and (2) achievement gaps between different schools (Bryk et al., 2010). The reasons for both types of gaps frequently overlap and include two general categories of causes—school-based causes and causes external to schools. The "Checklist of Possible Causes of Low Student Achievement" contains examples of both school-based and external causes.

This chapter focuses on school-based causes because they are the ones that principals and teachers are most likely to affect. First, however, it is necessary to review the causes of low achievement that derive from forces and conditions beyond the school.

Of all the external causes of low student achievement, poverty is the most widely recognized and the *root cause* of a variety of other external causes (Calkins et al., 2007). Parenting problems, for example, are frequently associated with the effects of marginal incomes. Poverty dictates where families live, typically urban neighborhoods and rural settings with high concentrations of other poor families, relatively few job opportunities, and underfunded schools. To make ends meet, parents often must work multiple jobs requiring them to travel considerable distances. As a consequence they have less time to spend with their children and less time to participate in school activities.

It is important to note, however, that all poor neighborhoods are not identical. When researchers studied Chicago elementary schools over an extended period of time, they found that schools posting consistently higher test scores drew students from neighborhoods that differed in important ways from the neighborhoods sending students to lower achieving schools (Bryk et al., 2010). All the neighborhoods were characterized by poverty, but the former had higher levels of religious participation, greater collective efficacy and connections with other parts of the city, and lower levels of crime and abused or neglected children than the latter neighborhoods.

Poverty is associated with parents' level of educational attainment. Mothers and fathers in low income and welfare-supported households are less likely to have completed high school or attended college. Parental level of education, in turn, is highly correlated with student success in school. Less-well-educated parents want their children to succeed in school, but they may lack the background and skills to reinforce academic habits and assist their children with school work. Furthermore, they typically lack the resources to provide their children with additional learning opportunities such as private tutors, music lessons, and vacations.

Children's health issues also are associated with poverty (Calkins et al., 2007). Children from low-income households are less likely to receive regular check-ups and nutritious meals. The health issues of these youngsters can be traced in many cases to poor health care during pregnancy and their mothers' unhealthy habits.

Living in impoverished neighborhoods and communities can expose young people to heightened levels of gang activity and substance abuse. These problems frequently spill over into schoolyards, classrooms, and corridors, presenting educators with enormous challenges. Peer culture also can undermine school achievement. Ogbu (2003) found that negative peer influence even can be a factor in relatively affluent communities. Many African American teenagers in his Shaker Heights, Ohio, study associated school academic success with "acting white." As a consequence they avoided Advanced Placement courses, questioned the benefits of doing well in school, and refrained from participating in class activities.

Poverty and its correlates are not the only external reasons why some schools are low performing. Schools exist in a political environment characterized by contentious issues and limited resources. The ability of educators to address students' academic needs effectively can be adversely affected by school board politics and inadequate funding. Strong district leadership sometimes can overcome these impediments, but unfortunately many low-performing school systems suffer from frequent turnover at the top. Principals are forced to adjust to a continuing parade of new superintendents, central office administrators, and school board members.

Poverty, parenting, peer influence, politics—all can negatively impact student achievement. While these causes must not be discounted, the focus of turnaround diagnostics should be the causes over which school personnel can exert some control. School-based causes often represent *mediating causes*. In other words, they may not be root causes, but addressing them actually can reduce or eliminate the effects of root causes.

Consider a student whose upbringing lacked access to a language- and literature-rich environment at home. These poverty-related deficits constitute root causes of low academic achievement. When the young person enters school, he is not exposed to reading programs that emphasize vocabulary development. Consequently the longer he attends school, the less able he is to understand written text. The school's failure to provide supplementary vocabulary development represents a mediating cause of low achievement. Had such assistance been provided early in the student's schooling, the negative impact of the root causes of his problem could have been reduced or eliminated.

The next section examines a variety of school-based causes and how they can be identified as part of the diagnostic process.

School-Based Causes

Iatrogenic medicine is a branch of medical practice devoted to treating problems *created* by those who provide medical care. Such problems can result from a variety of mistakes, from infections picked up in hospitals to undetected drug allergies. One of the greatest sources of iatrogenic problems, however, is the misdiagnosis of patient problems. The point for turnaround principles should be obvious. Misdiagnosing the causes of low achievement also can contribute to continued low achievement! A big part of medical training involves learning to ask patients the right questions. Unfortunately, programs that prepare principals do not always provide similar guidance.

Once principals understand their schools' achievement problems and related issues such as attendance and discipline, they can begin to zero in on possible school-based causes of the problems. To help focus inquiry, seven targets of causal investigation should be on every turnaround principal's agenda. The targets include personnel, programs, policies, processes, practices, professional development, and parental involvement and community partnerships. Each target is defined below.

1. *Personnel* is a large category that encompasses the qualifications of staff members, their track records in their present roles, school staffing arrangements, and the responsibilities associated with particular roles.
2. *Programs* are formal, school-based offerings that are intended to address academic and/or nonacademic needs. Programs may be comprehensive or specific to one area. Some programs are designed for preventive purposes while others constitute interventions. Curriculum programs include offerings for all students as well as supplementary offerings for subsets of students. A reading series is a program. So, too, is Responsive Classroom, Success for All, a ninth grade academy, and a summer enrichment course.
3. *Policies* refer to school-based rules, guidelines, and regulations (as opposed to formal, board-adopted mandates). Policies may address academic mat-

ters (i.e., grading, homework, make-up work), discipline, or personnel (i.e., co-teaching).

4. *Processes* concern organizational mechanisms that support the core functions of teaching and learning. Examples of processes include scheduling (adoption of a 4 × 4 block schedule), planning, data analysis, curriculum alignment, articulation across grade-levels, and personnel evaluation.

5. *Practices* refer to activities related directly to teaching and assessment that are expected of all or most teachers. Examples include inquiry-based teaching and interim testing in reading and math.

6. *Professional development* pertains to school-sponsored training that is required of all or most staff members and that focuses on school goals/needs.

7. *Parental involvement* and *community partnership* involve school-based efforts to initiate and strengthen relationships with parents and local organizations.

Suggestions of investigative questions for each target category are provided in this section. Some of the questions may seem too straightforward and obvious,

---

1. PERSONNEL

Are current faculty members qualified to teach their subject(s)?

Is there evidence that staff turnover has contributed to low achievement?

Have the strongest teachers been assigned to work with the weakest students?

Are there some staff members for whom the administration has low expectations?

How do specialists at the school spend their time?

Is there evidence that specialists are positively impacting student achievement?

but, as the saying goes, it is easier to ask dumb questions than to correct dumb mistakes. The answers to the questions should provide insights into the school-based causes of low student achievement.

There is considerable evidence that some teachers in low-performing schools lack the proper credentials to teach the subjects to which they have been assigned. Teaching content for which an individual is ill-prepared clearly can contribute to low student achievement. Even when teachers possess the proper credentials, however, they may not have kept up with advances in their content area. Looking carefully at previous evaluations of each faculty member should be on every principal's "to do" list. Evaluations, though, do not always accurately reflect a teacher's track record, so principals also need to look at the achievement of each teacher's students over the past few years. Judgments of teacher effectiveness always should take into account the achievement levels of students assigned to the teacher. Principals must be sensitive to the fact that certain teachers may be assigned larger numbers of lower-achieving students.

Low achievement also can be affected by staff turnover, a frequent problem with many struggling urban schools. The impact of turnover should be detectable by comparing the performance of students assigned to a new teacher with the performance of these students in previous coursework with experienced teachers.

Every faculty boasts some teachers with stronger track records than their colleagues. A principal needs to determine if these highly effective teachers spend at least part of each day working with struggling students. If low-achievers are routinely assigned to new teachers and less effective teachers, this fact can help account for low student achievement.

We know the adverse effects of low expectations for students. The same effects can result from low expectations for certain faculty members. Sometimes little is expected of teachers who are close to retirement or who have been assigned large numbers of challenging students. If it is unlikely that these teachers can be replaced, principals may decide to live with their low expectations, a decision that poorly serves the needs of students. Insights into expectations for teachers can be gleaned from teacher interviews, reviews of teacher evaluations, and past professional development plans for individual teachers.

Low-performing schools often are assigned a variety of specialists, including reading and math specialists, Title I teachers, instructional coaches, special education teachers, and teachers of English language learners. It is very important for principals to know how these individuals spend their time and whether there is evidence that students are benefitting from their presence at school. If specialists are not positively impacting student achievement, their roles should be redefined or they should be replaced. A similar analysis needs to be conducted for guidance counselors and any other noninstructional staff members who work with students.

Low-performing schools frequently operate a variety of programs intended to help students increase academic achievement and experience school success. Programs sometimes are built into the regular school schedule, such as Title I classes, sheltered classes for English language learners, double-blocked classes in language arts and mathematics, pre-Algebra classes, and Response to Intervention (RtI) offerings (Tier II and Tier III). There also are programs provided before and after school as well as on Saturdays and during the summer and intersessions (for year-round schools).

Special programs consume human and material resources. They require large amounts of student and teacher time. Principals need to know whether these programs are achieving their intended purposes. If they are not, programs should be adjusted or replaced. Unfortunately, programs are not

2. PROGRAMS

What programs are available for struggling students and students at risk of not advancing?

How effective are these programs?

How are students assigned to these programs?

Based on identified student needs, are there needs that currently are not being addressed programmatically?

Are programs representing the school's mainstream curriculum aligned with state and district standards and standardized tests?

always evaluated on a regular basis by school and district personnel. As a result, principals may need to collect their own data in order to determine the effectiveness of special programs.

One important aspect of special programs concerns how students are assigned to them. Are programs optional? Must students meet certain criteria or be referred by staff members? Principals need to find out whether some students who could benefit from special programs are not taking advantage of them and the reasons why. In the case of before and after-school programs and summer programs, transportation to and from school could be a problem. In the case of regular-school-day programs such as RtI Tier II and Tier III interventions, criteria for student placement may not always be applied consistently.

Most low-performing schools need a continuum of special programs to meet the various needs of struggling students as well as high achievers. Frequently, however, there may be programmatic gaps. A pre-Algebra class may be available, for example, but no pre-Geometry class. No supervised study hall may be provided during the school day for students who cannot complete homework at home. Students who fall behind in credit accumulation and therefore run the risk of not graduating may lack access to a summer credit-recovery program. Turnaround principals should conduct a gap analysis of student needs and the services currently available to address these needs.

Focusing on special programs is an important part of the diagnostic process, but so, too, is understanding regular school offerings. Case studies of low-performing schools frequently report that course content is not carefully aligned to state and district standards and the tests that are based on these standards. Principals should enlist the assistance of teachers and content specialists in order to determine how well aligned course content is to standards. One of the most noted school-based causes of low achievement is students' lack of exposure to subject matter on which they eventually are tested.

While school boards alone are empowered to promulgate formal policies governing district-wide matters, individual schools are permitted in many cases to create operational guidelines and informal policies governing such matters as homework, grading, discipline, grouping of students, and scheduling. These guidelines and policies sometimes can place certain students at a decided disadvantage when it comes to their academic progress. Consider a policy that automatically assigns a zero for work not turned in on time.

---

3. POLICIES

Are certain school policies associated with student failure?

Are school policies achieving the desired effects?

Are school policies enforced consistently?

Even if a student earns 100 on the next assignment, the average of a zero and 100 is 50, still a failing mark. In the face of such a policy, some students may simply give up.

A good school policy, as defined by Duke and Canady, is one "that increases the likelihood that school goals will be achieved without adversely affecting any particular group of students" (1991, p. 7). The diagnostic process therefore should include an examination of school guidelines and policies that may not be serving the interests of struggling and at-risk students. A policy, for example, that requires 25 percent of a student's grade to be based on homework may seem reasonable for students from middle-class homes. Students from poor households, however, may lack the necessary resources to do homework or even a proper place in which to do it. If these students are not given an opportunity to complete homework at school, they clearly are at a disadvantage.

A further concern involves the consistency with which school policies are enforced. Advocates for African American and Hispanic students frequently point to statistics that indicate minority students are far more likely to be suspended from school than white students, even when white students commit similar offenses. Turnaround principals must take a close look at school policies that may be enforced in a discriminatory manner. Such practices can discourage some students and send a message that they are not as valued as other students.

Processes include a variety of school-wide mechanisms intended to support the core functions of teaching and learning. Perhaps the most important of these mechanisms involve meetings of teachers and other professional

4. PROCESSES

Do teachers meet on a regular basis to analyze student achievement data, discuss interventions for struggling students, and develop common assessments?

What occurs following these meetings?

Are processes in place to monitor progress on school improvement plans?

Are processes in place to ensure that all students are registered and assigned to classes on the first day of school?

Do guidance personnel monitor all students to determine if they are on track to graduate?

Are processes in place for gathering student perceptions of their school experience?

staff. Such meetings can be devoted to a number of critical purposes, ranging from the analysis of student achievement data and the identification of particular students in need of additional assistance, to curriculum planning and the development of common assessments. In schools that have succeeded in turning around, these meetings occur on a regularly scheduled basis. Teacher leaders and administrators make it their business to follow up these meetings to see that decisions actually are implemented. Principals need to determine not only that teachers are meeting regularly but also that the meetings are accomplishing their intended purposes.

Similarly, processes should be in place for monitoring progress on the goals and objectives identified in the school's annual improvement plan. Most schools are required to develop such plans, but sometimes the plans are forgotten as soon as the school year begins. If goals and objectives are not being achieved, principals must find out the reasons why. It is likely that some of these reasons also can help to explain low student achievement.

In many low-performing schools, the first days of school can be chaotic. Some students are not registered and assigned to classes in a timely manner. These students may have to wait days or even weeks before their schedules are finalized. Getting off to such a bumpy start places these students at a decided disadvantage. Principals need to gather data on the processes in place to prevent such annual start-up problems.

Another problem that can have adverse effects for students is the failure of guidance personnel to track credit accumulation. I have found instances in low-performing schools where students are not told until their senior year that they lack sufficient credits to graduate. No process was in place to keep track of every student's academic progress. The diagnostic process should include a component about understanding how the guidance department functions and to what effect.

Much can be learned about the problems described above as well as additional school-related issues by regularly soliciting input from students. Successful turnaround principals keep in close touch with students through blogs, emails, surveys, student advisory groups, focus groups, exit interviews with departing students, and ad hoc meetings concerning particular issues. When Nancy Weisskopf was principal of South Hills High School in Fort Worth, Texas, she regularly hosted meetings of six to eight students to find out why they were struggling with particular course content. She videotaped these meetings so that the students' remarks could be shared later with her faculty. The diagnostic process should include data on all processes designed to obtain student perceptions of their school experience.

Classroom practices are the heart of the educational enterprise. Years of research on effective teaching and assessment have provided principals with clear guidelines regarding what to look and listen for when conducting classroom observations. Whether gathered through formal observations or frequent walkthroughs, observational data needs to be an integral part of the diagnostic process. It is hard to imagine a low-performing school where instructional practice is not an issue.

The questions listed in the Practices textbox represent some of the more important aspects of teaching practice on which principals can and should focus. The importance of clear and challenging expectations has been well established (Weinstein, 2002). Teachers convey expectations in various ways, from the kinds of questions they ask in class to the remarks they write on

---

5. PRACTICES

Are students informed about what they are expected to learn before instruction begins?

Are all students held to high expectations?

Do teachers employ a variety of teaching strategies and grouping formats?

Do teachers differentiate instruction in order to accommodate student needs?

Do teachers make regular use of sound assessment practices including interim or benchmark tests?

What steps do teachers take when students experience difficulty learning?

---

student work. While observations of teaching should provide vital information on how and what expectations are conveyed in class, students also have insights to offer on the subject.

Another well-established principle of good instruction concerns the methods used to promote learning. Students respond best when methods are varied and include opportunities for active learning and problem solving. Because students bring different learning needs to class, differentiated instruction also is an important dimension of effective teaching (Tomlinson, 2001). Dividing students into small groups provides a useful basis for such differentiation as do arrangements involving various classroom learning centers or stations. Principals need to be on the lookout, though, for teachers who always assign students to the same groups. Such a practice may not always be in the best interest of low achievers.

Schools typically are judged to be low performing based on how students do on annual high-stakes tests. While these measures can be helpful under certain circumstances, they are no substitute for daily classroom assessment and regular tests of student progress (Stiggins, 1997). Only by collecting frequent data on how well students are learning required content can teachers make the instructional adjustments necessary to ensure that all students continue to move forward. Lack of sound assessment practice clearly contributes to low achievement. Principals therefore need to know what assessment practices are being employed by teachers.

Principals also need to know what teachers do when assessments indicate that students are experiencing difficulties. Frequent classroom assessment alerts teachers that particular students need help, but it does not ensure that help is forthcoming. Even when assistance is provided, it may not necessarily be timely or effective assistance. The first line of defense against student failure is the classroom teacher. Schools fail when individual students fail, and schools only can be turned around one student at a time. Special education advocates understand this point, which is why special needs students are

6. PROFESSIONAL DEVELOPMENT

What professional development have current faculty members received, individually and together, during the last three years?

Has professional development focused on the data-based needs of students?

Has professional development been offered on a continuing basis, and have newly hired faculty members been brought up-to-date on previous training?

Are highly effective regular and special education teachers involved in providing professional development?

Do teachers have access to coaches with special expertise in areas where student achievement is low?

Is there evidence that professional development training is put to use in classrooms?

guaranteed timely and targeted assistance. Principals must find out if other struggling students are receiving the same quality of help.

It is a safe assumption that faculty members in low-performing schools can benefit from professional development as long as such training targets identified needs and is provided on an ongoing basis. One-shot workshops and training that addresses very general topics have not proved to make much of a difference in classroom practice or student achievement. It is also important to make provisions for giving newly hired faculty the same training that their colleagues already have received.

Often under-utilized sources of professional development are current faculty members who have been particularly effective working with struggling students. Special education teachers in particular have skills that should be shared with their regular education colleagues. Such sharing can occur in actual classroom settings as well as faculty gatherings devoted to professional development. Access to coaches with expertise in areas such as reading and mathematics remediation also can be a valuable resource.

Professional development is time-consuming and often costly. If it is not making a difference in student achievement, principals need to find out why. They also should follow up on trainings by seeing whether instructional practice actually is changing. Sometimes the training itself is inadequate or inappropriate. In other cases, however, teachers simply prefer to stick with their routines. Whatever the case, low-performing schools are unlikely to be turned around without a substantial amount of timely and targeted professional development that succeeds in altering instructional practice.

The support of parents and community groups can be a valuable component of school turnaround initiatives. When parents are kept up-to-date on how their children are doing in school and if they are on track to graduate, students are more likely to focus on school work and try to do their best. Parents and community groups can be important sources of school volunteers, supplementary resources, and special services. Low levels of parent and community involvement may not necessarily *cause* low student achievement, but they can be impediments to school improvement.

New principals need to find out as much as they can about prior efforts to build parent-school and community-school relations. Have some efforts been more successful than others? Under what circumstances have parents

7. PARENT INVOLVEMENT
AND COMMUNITY PARTNERSHIP

What efforts have been made to increase parent involvement in their children's schooling?

What partnerships have been formed with community groups, organizations, and agencies?

Have clear purposes for partnerships been articulated?

Do parents and community members support the school turnaround initiative?

and community groups been willing to support school improvement efforts? Have school leaders been clear about what purposes they wanted to accomplish through parent and community engagement? Parent and community partnerships sometimes fail because school personnel are too vague about the intended goals of such efforts.

DIAGNOSING THE CAUSES OF LOW ACHIEVEMENT
You have just reviewed a variety of questions that may need to be answered in order to obtain the data to determine school-based causes of low student achievement. Suggestions have been made about how to collect this data and from whom. Classroom walkthroughs and reviews of previous teacher evaluations, for example, are useful data sources. Students also can provide important information related to the causes of low achievement.

Once you have begun to accumulate data on personnel, programs, policies, processes, practices, professional development, parent involvement, and community partnerships, you may want to create a Diagnostic Matrix like the one in this section to facilitate the process of zeroing in on school-based causes. A Diagnostic Matrix helps to remind your colleagues and you that there are always multiple causes of low achievement. Having noted this, it also bears mentioning that you should not try to focus on all possible school-based causes at the same time.

—∞∞∞—

Turnaround Tip: The diagnostic process is supposed to help in identifying multiple school-based causes of low achievement and in choosing particular causes to focus on.

—∞∞∞—

If you look at the sample Diagnostic Matrix developed by a high school leadership team, you can see that an examination of data on student academic achievement, attendance, and behavior revealed six problems. Interviews with stakeholders, survey data, and a review of past school improvement plans then led to the identification of nine possible causes for these problems.

When the school's leadership team filled in the matrix, they discovered that two of the causes were checked for three different problems. Inexperienced teachers were assigned to teach Algebra 1, classes for English language learners and some special education students, and half of the classes for ninth graders. Leadership team members believed that teacher inexperience could help explain academic and behavior problems (high suspension rate).

A second possible cause for these three problem areas was found to be the lack of professional development that focused on Algebra instruction, English for ELLs and special education students, and how to handle behavior problems in ninth grade classes.

Based on their analysis, the leadership team concluded that a primary focus of their School Turnaround Plan needed to be targeted professional development in the areas of Algebra instruction, English for ELLs and special education students, and classroom management for ninth grade teachers. Other possible causes for identified problems would be addressed by the leadership team after targeted professional development had been implemented and its impact assessed.

The importance of "why." One of the most useful diagnostic tools is the one-word question, "Why?" It is especially helpful when it comes to distinguishing symptoms and causes. Imagine that you have identified a possible cause for a large number of failing grades by sixth graders at the end of the first grading period. You initially attribute the failing grades to the difficult transition from elementary school, a transition in which youngsters go from being big fish in a little pond, to being little fish in a big pond.

Table 3.2. Sample Diagnostic Matrix for a Low-Performing High School

Identified Problems	Possible School-Based Causes								
	Inexperienced teachers	Ineffective counseling	No "pathway" to graduation	Bullying by upperclassmen	Poor attendance at "help" sessions	Loss of two ELL teachers	Weak middle school math program	No targeted professional development	Poor home-school communications
High failure rate in Algebra 1 for all subgroups	√				√		√	√	
Low pass rate on state English test for ELLs and special ed. students	√				√	√		√	
Low % of Latino students in honors courses		√	√						√
Increasing dropout rate for Latino and Native American students		√	√			√			
High absenteeism rate for ninth graders					√				√
High suspension rate for ninth graders	√							√	

You ask yourself, "Why is the transition to sixth grade so rough this year?" After consulting your sixth grade teachers, you learn that current sixth graders were not accustomed to receiving grades for homework in elementary school. The reason why many of them received failing marks in sixth grade is that they did not turn in acceptable homework assignments.

Once again you ask, "Why?" You conclude that sixth grade teachers did not meet with elementary teachers to discuss their expectations for students in middle school. In addition, no mention of the importance of homework was made to students and their parents at the sixth grade orientation in August.

You get the idea. Every time you ask "Why?" and provide an answer, you come a bit closer to the root cause of a problem. Getting teachers to participate in the "Why?" exercise can be a valuable part of turnaround diagnostics. This process also can reveal fundamental differences among faculty members regarding the reasons for academic problems and related issues. Just remember that the purpose of the "Why?" exercise is to identify *school-based causes*, not causes over which educators exert little control.

When a root cause is traced to factors external to the school, a change in mindset is called for. Instead of adopting a cause-and-effect mindset, one that determines that nothing can be done by educators to eliminate external causes, it is preferable to adopt a challenge-and-response mindset. Poverty, for example, may be the root cause of low achievement for some students. So, what will be the *response* of school personnel to the *challenge* of poverty? Educators may not be able to eliminate poverty, but they can be trained to address the effects of poverty.

Event mapping. Another useful tool for diagnosing possible causes of academic problems is event mapping (Aladjem et al., 2010). Event maps include data on student achievement over a specified time period and important programmatic and personnel changes over the same time period. The following example of an event map for Jefferson Middle School illustrates the key features.

The top half of the event map tracks student performance on the eighth-grade state test in English from the fall of 2010 to the fall of 2014. The bottom half identifies programmatic and personnel changes for the same period. The objective is to identify possible causes for the change in slope of student performance from one year to the next. The jump from a 50 percent to a 72 percent pass rate between the fall of 2010 and the fall of 2011 could have been influenced, for example, by the appointment of a new principal. A slight drop the next year may have been the result of adopting a new eighth-grade English textbook and a change in the feeder system (redistricting) for the middle school. Two English teachers also retired in 2011.

The rebound in test scores in 2013 may have been due to teachers becoming more familiar with the new English textbook and the benchmark tests introduced the previous year. As for the big drop in scores in 2014, a change in the state eighth-grade English test seems a likely reason.

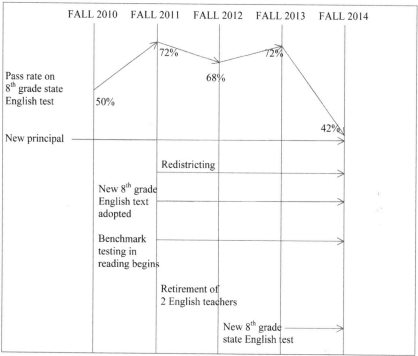

FIGURE 3.1
Event map, Jefferson Middle School.

Making use of event maps provides turnaround principals and their faculties with a useful picture of student achievement and school changes over
time. While event maps do not offer proof of low achievement, they permit
useful inferences to be drawn.

Predictors. In recent years, educational researchers have searched for student data that predicts subsequent problems. These predictors, or leading
indicators as they are sometimes called, are not necessarily causes per se, but
they are so highly correlated to negative outcomes such as dropping out of
high school that they are close to being causal.

In one Philadelphia study, researchers found four potent predictors, any
one of which predicted with 75 percent accuracy that a student would not
finish high school (Neild, Balfanz, and Herzog, 2007). The four predictors
were all based on a student's sixth grade record and included a failing grade in

mathematics, a failing grade in English, attendance below 80 percent for the year, and an "unsatisfactory" behavior mark in at least one class. Researchers in New York City have identified similar predictors of later academic problems as early as fourth grade (Kieffer, Marinell, and Stephenson, 2011).

Turnaround principals may not be able to conduct large scale statistical analyses in order to locate predictors, but they can examine the past school records of their students and determine if certain aspects of students' prior educational experiences are associated with subsequent academic problems. This information then can be used to initiate early warning systems and targeted interventions. If an absenteeism rate of 20 percent or more is predictive of dropping out, for example, principals need to intervene at the first sign of increasing absenteeism. Parents and students should be apprised of predictors so that they understand the likely consequences of allowing problems to go unaddressed.

ENGAGING STAKEHOLDERS

This chapter has addressed what principals can do to compile and analyze data for the purpose of diagnosing school-based causes of low achievement. It would be a mistake, however, to regard the diagnostic process as a solitary endeavor or even one reserved exclusively for a school leadership team. Gathering and interpreting data are processes that benefit from widespread participation. The more voices that are heard, the greater the likelihood of identifying school-based causes of low achievement.

An added benefit of broad-based participation in turnaround diagnostics is the effect it can have on the launching of a turnaround initiative. Staff, student, and community commitment to school improvement can be generated through the process of collecting and analyzing data. Individuals have a chance to share insights and feel valued. They begin to appreciate the value of working together even before the actual work of turning around a low-performing school commences. Turnaround principals are much more likely to build consensus and enlist support for their School Turnaround Plans when they have invited broad-based participation from the outset (Thompson et al., 2011).

Turnaround diagnostics have been discussed as a key element in the process of planning school turnarounds. To maximize the benefits of diagnostics, however, the search for school-based causes of academic problems needs to be ongoing. School administrators and teachers should get in the habit of identifying the causes of problems when the problems first arise.

NOTE

1. The "Checklist of Possible Causes of Low Student Achievement" is a valuable tool to use with teachers as they prepare to initiate a school turnaround project Compiling responses to the checklist provides a principal with some sense of what causes teachers believe they can and cannot impact.

REFERENCES

Aladjem, D. K.; Birman, B. F.; Orland, M.; Harr-Robins, J.; Heredia, A.; Parrish, T. B.; and Ruffini, S. J. 2010. *Achieving Dramatic School Improvement: An Exploratory Study.* Washington, DC: U.S. Department of Education.

Bryk, A. S.; Sebring, P. B.; Allensworth, E.; Luppescu, S.; and Easton, J. Q. 2010. *Organizing Schools for Improvement.* Chicago: University of Chicago Press.

Calkins, A.; Guenther, W.; Belfiore, G.; and Lash, D. 2007. *The Turnaround Challenge.* Boston: Mass Insight.

Duke, D. L. and Canady, R. L. 1991. *School Policy.* New York: McGraw-Hill.

Kieffer, M. J.; Marinell, W. H.; and Stephenson, N. S. 2011. *The Middle Grades Student Transitions Study. Working Brief.* New York: The Research Alliance for New York City Schools.

Murphy, J. 2010. *The Educator's Handbook for Understanding and Closing Achievement Gaps.* Thousand Oaks, CA: Corwin.

Neild, R. C.; Balfanz, R.; and Herzog, L. 2007. An early warning system. *Educational Leadership*, 65(2), 28–33.

Ogbu, J. U. 2003. *Black American Students in an Affluent Suburb.* Mahwah, NJ: Earlbaum.

Payne, C. M. 2008. *So Much Reform, So Little Change.* Cambridge, MA: Harvard Education Press.

Stiggins, R. J. 1997. *Student-Centered Classroom Assessment,* 2nd ed. Upper Saddle River, NJ: Merrill.

Stone, D. 1989. Causal stories and the formation of policy agendas. *Political Science Quarterly,* 104(2), 281–300.

Tomlinson, C. A. 2001. *How to Differentiate Instruction in Mixed-Ability Classrooms,* 2nd ed. Alexandria, VA: ASCD.

Thompson, C. L.; Brown, K. M.; Townsend, L. W.; Henry, G. T.; and Fortner, C. K. 2011. *Turning Around North Carolina's Lowest Achieving Schools (2006–2010).* Chapel Hill, NC: Consortium for Educational Research and Evaluation—North Carolina.

Weinstein, R. S. 2002. *Reaching Higher.* Cambridge, MA: Harvard University Press.

4

Planning for the Short Term and the Long Run

Leaders of low-performing schools are expected to invest considerable time and energy in planning for school improvement. Most states and school districts require principals to oversee the development of an annual plan specifying measurable improvement goals and the means for achieving them. Chronically low-performing schools receiving federal School Improvement Grants and Title I aid must have plans for raising student achievement and reducing the achievement gaps between student subgroups. These plans represent one of the primary mechanisms for holding school leaders accountable and monitoring school turnaround efforts.

The prescribed templates for annual plans—henceforth referred to as School Turnaround Plans (STP)—do not vary a great deal from district to district and state to state. An STP typically involves a series of goals, objectives, strategies, and timelines. Despite these commonalities, STPs can vary greatly in quality and effectiveness. Some plans are so poorly designed that they stand little chance of raising student achievement. Studies of school improvement plans have found many to be "unrealistically comprehensive, overloaded with activities, and full of minutiae rather than being focused and strategic" (Mintrop, MacLellan, and Quintero, 2001, p. 200).

Other plans may be well designed, but they are not implemented well or they are quickly forgotten once the school year begins. In this chapter and the next you will read about how to design a School Turnaround Plan with a good chance of success. Later in the book, keys to effective implementation of plans will be addressed.

The previous two chapters laid the groundwork for sound planning by examining how to target student academic needs and diagnose the school-based causes of low student achievement. These two activities should be sufficient to generate a sense of urgency for change, assuming that various stakeholders have an opportunity to participate and express their concerns. Once a sense of urgency has been generated, the next step in leading the change process, according to Kotter (1996), involves building a guiding coalition. This calls for putting together a group with enough influence to direct the change process, and ensuring that the group works together as a team.

It is my contention that the initial planning process for an STP provides an ideal opportunity to begin building a guiding coalition. In order to take advantage of this opportunity, however, a turnaround principal must consider carefully who should be involved in the planning process. Newly appointed principals, of course, will find the choice of participants more challenging, since they are unlikely to know who they can count on.

A great deal of attention in the literature is devoted to the School Turnaround Plan itself, including its format and content. While such a plan can be an important improvement tool and source of guidance, it is *planning*, more than *a plan*, that holds the key to school turnaround. Put differently, planning should be regarded as a continuous process, not a once-a-year activity leading to the development of a School Turnaround Plan.

———

Turnaround Tip: The focus of the turnaround process should be on continuous planning rather than the annual development of a School Turnaround Plan.

———

This chapter takes a close look at both short-term and long-term planning. Short-term planning is best conducted in ninety-day segments. Long-term planning addresses what stakeholders agree should be the vision for their school. Short-term planning is oriented to identifying and eliminating or reducing problems that stand in the way of academic improvement. Long-term planning, on the other hand, looks beyond required achievement gains to the creation of a school of which the community can be proud. Before addressing short-term and long-term planning, however, it is necessary to think about the participants in the planning process.

WHO SHOULD BE INVOLVED IN PLANNING?

Participation in short-term planning is a complex matter because planning consists of different components. First comes the input stage when the data on which a plan will be based is collected. Next comes the actual development of a School Turnaround Plan. Obtaining reactions to the draft STP represents a third stage of the process. Based on these reactions, the draft plan may be adjusted. Then the plan must be approved. The individuals involved in each of these stages may vary, depending on district policy, local expectations, and the leadership style of the principal.

Opportunities for Participation in Turnaround Planning
1. Pre-planning input
2. Development of a draft plan
3. Reactions to the draft plan
4. Approval of the plan

In the gathering of preplanning input, it is generally a good idea to cast a wide net. All stakeholder groups—parents, students, community members, school faculty, and district personnel—have a vested interest in the success of the turnaround process. They also may have important insights to share regarding why the school is low achieving and how improvements can be made. Turnaround principals should never assume that they know what stakeholders are thinking.

A word of caution is in order regarding the gathering of input for the planning process. Once people have been asked to share their perceptions, they are likely to want to be kept informed about the planning process. They also may expect their suggestions to be heeded. Keeping informants apprised of planning developments—what is often called *transparency*—is therefore important, as is explaining why particular suggestions were not incorporated into the plan.

When it comes to developing a draft School Turnaround Plan, the number of participants should be relatively small compared to the number of individuals providing preplanning input. There are cases, of course, where a turnaround principal may be the only person involved, but such solitary planning is not advisable.

When an STP is created by a school leadership team or a representative body of stakeholders, the likelihood of gaining acceptance of the plan increases. But there also are risks. Whenever there is more than one planner, the possibility of disagreement grows. Trying to appease opposing positions on particular planning issues can lead to a watered down plan that lacks the bold steps needed to achieve true turnaround. To avoid such problems, the principal must carefully manage the planning process.

The membership of planning groups typically includes both school administrators and teachers. Teachers may be appointed by the principal or elected by the faculty. Ideally, teacher participants will have expertise working with struggling students and a willingness to challenge conventional practice. Planning groups also may include parent and community representatives as well as district officials. In most cases, the principal serves as the chair of the group.

Once the planning group develops a draft School Turnaround Plan, the plan can be shared with stakeholders in order to obtain reactions and suggestions for modifications. Doing so alerts people to what the planning group is thinking and increases the chances that the final version of the STP will be accepted. Soliciting reactions to the draft plan, however, is not the same as voting on whether or not to approve the plan. The final decision on the STP should be made by the planning group. The district superintendent or school board may have to give final approval for the plan.

Because planning is best regarded as a continuous process, the planning group should not be disbanded once the STP has been approved. By continuing to meet and monitor the STP, the group can make adjustments as needed. Working on a series of 90-day plans rather than one annual plan facilitates the continuous planning process by ensuring regular reviews of progress and mid-course corrections when necessary. In the next section you will learn more about the elements that make up a 90-day plan.

SHORT-TERM PLANNING

Students of organizational effectiveness like to extol the virtues of vision—an image of what the organization is striving to be. Vision has its place in the school turnaround process as well, as you will see in the following section, but vision is no substitute for a clear and focused set of "next steps." Concentrating too soon on the ultimate destination can leave people wondering how they will ever get there. Educators in a low-performing school need to accumulate some short-term successes so that they have the momentum and confidence to press forward toward long-term goals.

One way to increase the chances for short-term successes is to conduct planning in ninety-day segments (Duke, Carr, and Sterrett, 2013). The University of Virginia's School Turnaround Program, one of the first programs to train leaders for low-performing schools, borrowed the idea of quarterly planning from the business community. Businesses have found that setting quarterly goals provides employees with more focused and manageable targets. In addition, when the only plan is a yearly plan, people often wait until the end of the year to assess progress and make adjustments. Waiting so long to correct a School Turnaround Plan can jeopardize the academic progress of many students. With a 90-day plan and a commitment to continuous planning, mid-course corrections can be made in a timely manner, thereby enabling ineffective strategies to be modified or scrapped and permitting teachers and students to get back on track.

Turnaround Tip: Organize the planning process around a series of 90-day plans.

One possible arrangement for continuous planning might entail a series of 90-day plans, beginning with a plan for the summer months (June, July, and August), followed by plans for September through November, December through February, and March through May. Each plan builds on what was (or was not) accomplished in the preceding plan. A set of overarching annual goals can serve as the foundation for the 90-day plans.

During the summer months the plan might involve assessing academic performance during the previous school year, diagnosing probable school-based causes of low achievement, and devising a plan to address some of these causes. Implementing this plan then becomes the focus for the next ninety days. In late November, the planning group reviews progress during the first semester and decides whether or not to alter elements of the fall plan and add additional goals. This process is repeated at the end of February.

Continuous planning represents a shift in school culture, so it may take a year or more for veteran staff members to accustom themselves to it. Ultimately, though, most educators embrace the process because they either see the benefits of a plan or they improve it before too much forward momentum has been lost. Fidelity to a plan makes little sense if students are not benefitting.

Components of a School Turnaround Plan. Plans consist of goals, objectives, strategies, and timelines. They also may include the resources needed to accomplish objectives and the individuals responsible for accomplishing them.

A goal is usually an ambitious target, one requiring a relatively long time to accomplish. Making progress on a goal requires achieving various objectives. Objectives are measurable, more focused than goals, and require less time to accomplish, as indicated by the following example in table 4.1:

Accomplishing each objective requires the implementation of one or more strategies (sometimes referred to as actions or interventions). Educators in low-performing schools, as a rule, should not plan to use strategies unless there is evidence that they work. Consider Objective 2 from the table. Strategies that have been shown to increase the pass rate in Algebra 1 include doubling the time for Algebra 1, timely tutoring, and greater emphasis on problem solving (Protheroe, 2007). It is a good idea to limit the number of

Table 4.1.

Goal	Objectives
Reduce the number of students retained in ninth grade by 50%.	Obj. 1: Reduce ninth grade absenteeism in the first quarter by 30%. Obj. 2: Reduce the percentage of ninth graders getting a "D" or "F" in Algebra 1 by 25%. Obj. 3: Increase the number of ninth graders participating in extracurricular activities by 20%.

strategies for a particular objective. One or two strategies at a time increases the likelihood of successful implementation.

Table 4.2 illustrates the range of strategies presented in the school improvement plans of thirteen low-performing Florida high schools.[1] Each of the high schools was required by the Florida Department of Education to have goals related to reading achievement. You can see that the number of strategies range from one at Butler and Crandell to twelve at Darnell. Ensuring the effective implementation of twelve reading strategies over one school year (nine months) would be a challenge for even the most capable principal, especially when Florida requires goals in a variety of other areas.

For each strategy, a timeline should be developed. The timeline helps those individuals charged with implementing the strategy as well as the group monitoring progress on achieving the objective. Principals also are advised to create a "master timeline" or calendar so that they can see at a glance when each strategy should be implemented and each objective should be achieved.

In order to implement a strategy, certain resources may be required. Possible resources include professional development, curriculum materials, technology, and additional personnel. Once strategies for each objective in the 90-day plan have been specified and necessary resources identified, the principal should compile a budget. A comprehensive budget then becomes a basis for negotiations with school district authorities and other funding sources.

One individual, typically a faculty member, should be placed in charge of implementing each objective. They should be noted in the 90-day plan. This individual functions as a project manager, bringing together a team of people to implement a strategy and periodically reporting on progress to the principal. Principals should not manage the implementation of any strategy, but instead serve as the person who receives reports from each project manager. A more in-depth discussion of project management appears in chapter 7.

A sample segment of a 90-day plan (table 4.3) is provided to give you an idea of what one might look like. The long-term goal is to cut in half the number of student suspensions. The diagnostic process revealed the fact that a large proportion of suspensions occurred because students who had been referred to the principal for discipline problems and assigned to after-school detention hall failed to show up. The consequence for missing detention at the school was an automatic suspension.

Table 4.2.   School Improvement Plan Strategies to Raise Reading Achievement for Thirteen Florida High Schools

Strategies	Avon	Butler	Crandell	Darnell	Edsel	Fruitland	Galago	Holden	Inverness	Joplin	Konley	Ludlow	Munson
I. Assessment & Monitoring													
Diagnostic testing to identify students in need of intervention	✓		✓										✓
Interim testing aligned to state tests	✓	✓									✓		
Monitoring of students who fail in first quarter											✓		
Classroom walkthroughs to monitor reading initiatives	✓												
II. Reading Programs & Materials													
Leveled texts in core subjects	✓												
Classroom libraries geared to student interests and reading levels				✓								✓	
Accelerated Reader program				✓							✓		
Coordinated implementation of district reading program	✓											✓	
School-wide campaign to promote reading									✓				
III. Initiatives to Support Reading Improvement													
Positive Behavior Support program	✓												
Rewards for students who achieve and/or behave appropriately	✓			✓									
Common planning of reading lessons					✓								
IV. Reading Instruction (in general) Special instructional focus on:													
Comprehension					✓					✓			
Fluency										✓		✓	

	1	2	3	4	5	6	7
Vocabulary				✓			
Test taking strategies	✓						
Use of context clues			✓				
Decoding skills			✓				
Identification of text structures			✓				
Recognition of different types of questions			✓				
Devel. of "reading stamina"	✓						
Use of CLOZE technique				✓			
Selective underlining & marginal notes			✓				
Use of graphic organizers to help students: Develop vocabulary		✓					
Recognize text structures				✓			
Summarize texts				✓			
Special instructional methods: Audio books				✓			
Choral reading				✓			
Discovery probes	✓						
Mini-focus lessons	✓						
Paired reading				✓			
Readers theater				✓			
Use various methods to activate background knowledge			✓	✓			
Use various methods to model analysis & synthesis of information				✓			
Provide students with choice of reading materials			✓				

(continued)

Table 4.2. *(continued)*

Strategies	Avon	Butler	Crandell	Darnell	Edsel	Fruitland	Galago	Holden	Inverness	Joplin	Konley	Ludlow	Munson
V. Special Assistance for struggling readers													
Tutoring—during school	✓								✓				
Tutoring—after school									✓				
Student conferences													
ACT Prep program (after school)											✓		
Use of AVID strategies (such as Cornell note-taking)											✓		
Use of ESOL and Migrant Ed. staff to help students (pullout program)											✓		
VI. Classroom Organization and Grouping													
Student groups based on reading level													✓
Formation of "literary groups"				✓									
Small group rotation system												✓	
Collaborative small group centers				✓									

	1	2	3	4	5	6	7
Assignment of fluent students to appropriate reading class	✓						
Assign ninth graders to small learning communities		✓					
Classroom listening stations based on reading level and student interest						✓	
VII. Scheduling/Time Use							
Uninterrupted time for reading			✓				
Double-block reading for struggling readers	✓						
Develop Instructional Focus Calendar for reading		✓					
"Skill block" days to address readiness for state testing			✓				
VIII. Professional Development							
P.D. to support reading program implementation				✓		✓	
P.D. on effective reading instruction				✓			
P.D. plans on improved reading instruction for every teacher							✓
IX. Parent & Community Involvement							
Parent phone calls					✓		
Parent/community recognition program for students						✓	

Table 4.3. 90-Day Plan Segment

Goal: Reduce suspensions for disciplinary reasons by 50%				
Objective: Reduce discipline referrals by 25% compared to the same period last school year	**1st Week of School 8/19–23**	**2nd Week 8/26–30**	**3rd Week 9/3–6**	**4th Week 9/9–13**
Strategy 1: Develop a set of school wide rules and consequences Tasks 1. Collect input from students on potential school rules (week 1) 2. Formulate schoolwide rules (week 1) 3. Develop consequences (week 1) 4. Share rules and consequences with faculty (week 1)	Tasks 1–4 were completed on schedule.			
Strategy 2: Teach new schoolwide rules and consequences to students Tasks 1. Provide direct instruction on school rules (weeks 1 and 2) 2. Students work in small groups to develop video or posters to demonstrate the school rules (week 2) 3. Test students on the rules (week 3) students who fail the test most spend their free period in study hall		Task 1 was completed on schedule; but students took longer than expected to complete their work on Task 2 and so it was extended to week 5.	• Task 3 was completed on schedule. • Task 4 was completed on schedule; the study hall will be housed in the 200 Building, in room 205. It will be open periods 1–6.	

The planning group reasoned that suspensions could be reduced if fewer students were referred to the principal for misconduct. To accomplish this objective, the initial 90-day plan focused on two strategies: (1) the development of a set of schoolwide rules and consequences, and (2) student instruction in the new rules and consequences. Several tasks were specified under each strategy. Some planning guides prefer for tasks to be listed in a separate action plan. Action plans will be addressed later in the book.

The timeline that was developed for this segment of a 90-day plan initially was left blank. As each task was accomplished, it was noted on the plan's template. As you can see, most of the tasks were completed on schedule. Once school rules were developed, the focus shifted to teaching rules to students. Besides direct instruction, a student-created video illustrating each rule was shown to students. Students then were given a test on the rules and consequences for breaking them. Students who passed the test were allowed to go to a "conversation area" in the cafeteria, work out in the gym, or spend time in the media center. Students who did not pass the test were required to remain in study hall. They were given one more chance to pass the test.

You can see that this segment of a School Turnaround Plan is very specific when it comes to the steps needed to achieve the objective—a 25 percent reduction in disciplinary referrals. Little guesswork is required to implement the plan, and the number of tasks appears manageable.

Focus, focus, focus. School Turnaround Plans fail for many reasons, none so predictable as trying to address too many goals in too short a time. Once a planning group has identified the school-based causes of academic problems, the temptation is great to address them all in the first 90-day plan. Individuals will lobby for their "pet" concern. Principals must be willing to intervene on behalf of a focused and manageable plan. The stakeholders in a low-performing school do not need to fail by using a well-intentioned but overly ambitious plan, thereby exacerbating an already problem-plagued situation.

Successful school turnarounds are characterized by *focus* (Duke, 2010). Focus is important at various stages of the turnaround process. The diagram below illustrates the points where focus is critical. It begins with the diagnostic process and the identification of a variety of academic problems. Agreeing on a few problems to focus on becomes the first order of business. Each problem is likely to derive from multiple causes. Planners must decide which

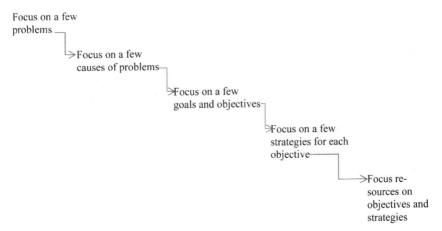

FIGURE 4.1
A focused approach to school turnaround.

causes the faculty is most likely to impact. Then they need to agree on a few goals to focus on during the first ninety days of the turnaround initiative. For each goal, several promising strategies should be chosen. Available resources then should be focused on implementing these strategies. There is no benefit to spreading resources so thinly over a wide variety of goals and strategies that little progress is likely.

If you led a planning group in the development of a School Turnaround Plan, you would be well served by employing a process for prioritizing the various problems that were identified during the initial stages of data analysis. I created such an instrument to help with this process as part of the Florida Turnaround Leaders Program (Duke, 2014).

The "Preliminary Assessment of Planning Priorities" (PAPP), as the instrument is titled, involves four steps. Step 1 requires that each member of the planning group independently list all the problems that they believe must be addressed in order to raise student achievement. This list can include external as well as school-based problems. The second step calls for members of the planning group to compare their individual lists of problems and develop a single list of problems identified by two or more individuals. A rating form then should be created. Problems are listed down the left-hand side of the form. Space for seven ratings per problem should be made across the top (see table 4.4).

Table 4.4. Preliminary Assessment of Planning Priorities
Worksheet for Group Planning

Potential Problems to Be Addressed in the School Turnaround Plan	A	B	C	D	E	F	G	TOTAL
1.								
2.								
3.								
4.								
5.								
6.								
7.								
8.								
9.								
10.								
11.								
12.								

Step 3 involves rating each problem on seven qualities, including impact, urgency, causation, competence, commitment, capacity, and prognosis (see accompanying rating scales).

Once individuals have rated each problem and calculated a total score (the sum of the seven ratings) for each problem, an average score is tabulated for each problem by adding all the individual total scores for each problem and dividing by the number of members of the planning group. The highest scores represent the priority problems that should be considered first.

Self-inflicted wounds. Developing and implementing a School Turnaround Plan is hard enough without making avoidable mistakes in the planning process. One such mistake—tackling too many goals and objectives in one plan—already has been noted, and others can be added to the list. Below are some of the more common planning mistakes. Problems affecting the implementation of plans will be discussed later in the book.

Table 4.5. Preliminary Assessment of Planning Priorities

Developed by Prof. Daniel L. Duke
University of Virginia

The purpose of this instrument is to assist School Turnaround Planning Teams in the process of prioritizing issues that need to be addressed. Issues include problems and concerns that stand in the way of higher student achievement. Individuals should examine each issue and rate it according to the scales below.

Rating Scales

A. IMPACT: This issue is likely to impact

4 – all students.
3 – most students.
2 – a few students.
1 – no students.

B. URGENCY: Failure to address this issue in the very near future is likely to have

4 – a major negative impact.
3 – a moderate negative impact.
2 – a modest negative impact.
1 – little or no negative impact.

C. CAUSATION: The cause(s) of this issue is(are) one(s) that school personnel have the authority to address

4 – without any outside assistance.
3 – without very much outside assistance.
2 – with some outside assistance.
1 – with a substantial amount of outside assistance.

D. COMPETENCE: The knowledge and skills to address the issue effectively are possessed by

4 – all current school personnel.
3 – most current school personnel.
2 – some current school personnel.
1 – few if any current school personnel.

E. COMMITMENT: The willingness to address the issue is likely for

4 – all current school personnel.
3 – most current school personnel.
2 – some current school personnel.
1 – few if any current school personnel.

F. CAPACITY: School personnel are likely to have access to

4 – all the resources needed to address the issue.
3 – most of the resources needed to address the issue.
2 – some of the resources needed to address the issue.
1 – few if any of the resources needed to address the issue.

G. PROGNOSIS: The likelihood that this issue can be addressed successfully over the coming school year is

4 – certain.
3 – probable.
2 – unlikely.
1 – nonexistent.

Impact concerns the number of students who are likely to benefit from correcting the problem.

Urgency pertains to the consequences of not making the problem a high priority.

Causation involves the source of the problem—either school-based or external to the school—and the authority to address it.

Competence refers to how well the current staff is equipped to address the problem.

Commitment refers to how willing the current staff is to address the problem.

Prognosis calls for a judgment of the likelihood that the problem can be addressed successfully.

Avoidable Planning Mistakes

- Selecting goals and objectives that cannot be measured
- Underestimating training needs
- Underestimating the resources needed to implement the plan
- Adopting unproven strategies
- Always adding to existing programs
- Creating unrealistic timelines

The goals and objectives that make up a School Turnaround Plan should be written in ways that enable planners to determine when, and if, they are achieved. Holding individuals accountable for making a good faith effort to achieve goals and objectives becomes difficult when subjective judgments are the only way to assess progress. Examples of measurable goals and objectives include the following:

- The gap in pass rates on the state eighth grade science test between African American and white students will be reduced by 30 percent.
- The number of ninth grade students receiving at least one out-of-school suspension will be reduced by 15 percent
- All fourth grade teachers will participate in the district-sponsored training on reading comprehension.
- Each department chair will conduct three walkthrough observations a week and provide feedback to each teacher within twenty-four hours.

Unsuccessful plans sometimes include strategies for such functions as aligning curriculum, data-driven decision making, and assisting struggling students without specifying when and how staff members will receive the training necessary to implement the strategies. It should never be assumed that individuals already possess the knowledge and skills to implement a strategy. Training increases the likelihood that the strategies to be implemented conform to guidelines and expectations. Provisions also should be made to train staff members who join the faculty after the original training has been completed.

Training typically requires resources. Materials must be purchased. Trainers need to be paid. Teachers must be reimbursed if training occurs outside of contracted hours. Additional resources may be required to accomplish other components of School Turnaround Plans. Sometimes more staff members are called for. Technical assistance may be needed to implement data management systems. Some objectives may involve the acquisition of technology and software. Planners must specify immediate resource needs as well as anticipate needs that are likely to arise down the road. In the case of new technology, for example, planners should budget not only for new equipment, but also for future maintenance and upgrades. Few things can frustrate staff members more than seeing a School Turnaround Plan stall because insufficient resources were budgeted.

Another concern when developing plans involves the choice of strategies. When planners choose strategies that lack evidence of effectiveness, resources can be wasted and students placed at risk. If research on the effectiveness of a particular strategy is unavailable, planners at least should identify schools in which the strategy has been implemented with some success.

It also is important to avoid implementing too many strategies at the same time or for the same objective. It is much more useful to focus on one strategy at a time, implement it with fidelity, and determine whether it makes a constructive contribution before moving on to additional strategies. When multiple strategies are implemented at the same time and desired outcomes are not achieved, it is difficult to determine the reasons why. Perhaps a particular strategy was poorly implemented or ill suited to the objective. Or maybe teachers were simply overwhelmed and confused by the combination of strategies. As in so many things, less can be more when it comes to school turnaround planning.

When developing plans, it is tempting for planners to do more adding than subtracting. Strategies typically involve new programs, policies, processes, practices, and so on. It can be just as important, however, for planners to call for the elimination of things. Doing away with programs and practices that are not working, for instance, can free up resources, personnel, and time so that greater attention will be focused on new initiatives. Plans that call for subtracting as well as adding also are more likely to be embraced by staff members.

The curse of many a failed School Turnaround Plan is an unrealistic time-line. Turnaround principals, of course, are expected to make quick and dramatic improvements, so the temptation to set short timelines for achieving objectives is great. It is of little value, however, to rush implementation and thereby reduce the chances for success. This is where good judgment on the part of principals is critical. Principals need to assess the existing demands on staff members and their capacity to tackle additional tasks. They also should determine what supplementary assistance can be provided by the school district before timelines are finalized.

Conducting the short-term planning needed to launch the school turn-around process is largely a matter of problem finding and problem solving. Emphasis is placed on eliminating or reducing the school-based causes of low achievement and removing the barriers to improvement. There is another type of planning, though, that is equally important, but that focuses on creating rather than eliminating. Long-term planning's purpose is to provide a vision of what a low-performing school ultimately can become.

PLANNING BEYOND TURNAROUND

Focus is the key to short-term planning, but by zeroing in on a manageable set of high priority goals, planners can leave some stakeholders wondering when their pet concerns will be addressed. One benefit of a long-term plan therefore is the assurance it provides that additional goals of importance eventually will be addressed. A long-term plan need not be as highly structured and detailed as a 90-day plan because circumstances will change over time and possibly result in modifications to long-range goals, but such plans should be public documents so that stakeholders understand how goals have been sequenced for future consideration. Put differently, a long-term plan is more of a design than a blueprint.

A second benefit of long-term planning involves the development of a vision that encompasses more than raising test scores. Identifying and overcoming academic problems may be the starting point for school turnaround, but the discovery of possibilities beyond turnaround is what will matter the most in the long run. Fritz captured the distinction in the following excerpt:

> The problem solvers propose elaborate schemes to define the problem, generate alternative solutions, and put the best solution into practice. If this process is successful, you might eliminate the problem. Then what you have is the absence of the problem you are solving. But what you do not have is the presence of a result you want to create. (Fritz, 1989, p. 31)

Perhaps the analogy of buying land and building a house clarifies the distinction between problem solving and creating. Before you build the house, you have to clear the land. Clearing the land is like problem solving. But before you clear the land, you need to have a design in mind for the house. Otherwise, you cannot make the appropriate changes to the landscape on which the house will sit.

The design is the vision of what the school can become. Arresting a downward trend in student achievement and beginning to raise scores on standardized tests and close achievement gaps are actions that promise to eliminate a school's placement in "improvement status." A certain amount of momentum can be gained by doing so. But creating an inspiring design has the potential to rally widespread support and engage the long-term commitment of the community. The ultimate purpose of long-term planning is to sustain the momentum gained during the initial phase of the turnaround process and continue to improve student outcomes.

In thinking about a long-term design, planners have three basic options. They can employ relatively *conventional* strategies to raise achievement to acceptable levels, thereby removing the threat of sanctions and matching the performance of benchmark schools. A variety of conventional strategies, including curriculum alignment and targeted professional development, will be discussed in the next chapter. The first option is often found when educators and community members want to restore a declining school to its previous position of local respect.

Alternatively, principals can employ *unconventional* strategies to raise achievement to acceptable levels, thereby removing the threat of sanctions and matching the performance of benchmark schools. Reconstituting low-performing schools by replacing a large percentage of teachers as well as the principal is one example of the second option. So, too, is closing the school and reopening it as a charter school.

The third option calls for the use of *unconventional* strategies to create an *unconventional* school, a school that not only exits "improvement status" but that provides an exciting new learning environment for students.

Elsewhere I have described a school that epitomized the third option (Duke, 2010). The school came about because a pair of visionary educational leaders in Franklin County, Virginia, were concerned about the high dropout rate in their high school. When they looked more deeply into the problem, they found that many eighth graders were making decisions that eventually led them to drop out. These students began to miss more days of school and disengage from academic work. Their interests shifted to finding after-school jobs and taking less challenging courses.

The opportunity for a turnaround came when voters approved a bond issue for a new middle school, but for only half of the requested funds to build a school that could accommodate all the middle school students in the county. Instead of waiting to submit a new bond request the following year, the superintendent and assistant superintendent decided to take the money and build a facility that could accommodate half the eighth graders in the county—roughly four hundred students. Their idea was for four hundred eighth graders to spend first semester at the new facility, then return for second semester to the old middle school (which was scheduled to be refurbished) while the other four hundred eighth graders came to the new facility. All sixth and seventh graders would continue to attend the old middle school.

Understanding that eighth graders found academic work uninspiring, the two educational leaders formed a coalition of community members and teachers who supported the design of a totally different kind of learning environment, one that did not look or function like a conventional school. Instead, the Center for Applied Technology and Career Exploration (CATCE) was designed to resemble a high-tech workplace. Its purpose was to expose students to a variety of careers, including those that required a college education and others that required only a high school diploma.

CATCE offered students eight career program options, ranging from natural resources and environmental protection, to health, medicine, and human services. Each career program, or module, was designed to run for thirty school days. Students chose three modules to cover the semester they attended CATCE. Instead of moving from one class to another, students spent all day in their module working on a project devised by their teachers. Two teachers taught each module. One teacher was a certificated teacher in a content area, while the second teacher came from the occupational area covered in the module. The natural resources and environmental protection module, for example, was co-taught by a biology teacher and a former member of the state forestry department.

To get students excited about the career focus of each module, teachers identified a real-world project that addressed a local concern or problem. Students in the natural resources and environmental protection module might investigate a toxic spill in a Franklin County stream. Over the course of thirty days they collected water samples from the stream, analyzed them, determined how to clean up the stream, and presented their recommendations to local authorities.

Eighth graders covered some of the state standards during their time at CATCE and the remainder during their semester back at the traditional middle school. By coming up with an unconventional design, Franklin County educators not only provided students with a rich array of career-oriented experiences, but they also raised student achievement and reduced the high school dropout rate.

Turnaround principals understand that they must figure out how to improve student performance on state standardized tests. Raising test scores, however, must never be viewed as an end in itself. The question that principals of low-performing schools and stakeholders need to address is this: Toward what ends are higher test scores supposed to contribute? Franklin County educators and community members agreed that making more students college and career ready was a worthy goal, and they came up with a design to achieve it.

Leaders of low-performing schools easily can get caught up in short-term planning—reducing discipline problems, closing achievement gaps, improving scores on reading tests, and the like. Their leadership, after all, will be judged according to whether or not rapid, measurable progress is made. Ultimately, however, the welfare of the community and its young people also requires an inspiring vision of what a low-performing school eventually can become and the long-term planning to achieve it.

NOTE

1. I compiled this list of strategies for the Florida Turnaround Leaders Program. All the high school names have been changed.

REFERENCES

Duke, D. L. 2014. A bold approach to the preparation of turnaround principals. *Management in Education*, 28(3), 80–85.

Duke, D. L. 2010. *Differentiating School Leadership*. Thousand Oaks, CA: Corwin.

Duke, D. L.; Carr, M.; and Sterrett, W. 2013. *The School Improvement Planning Handbook*. Lanham, MD: Rowman & Littlefield.

Fritz, R. 1989. *The Path of Least Resistance*. New York: Fawcett Columbine.

Kotter, J. P. 1996. *Leading Change*. Boston: Harvard Business School Press.

Mintrop, H.; MacLellan, A. M.; and Quintero, M. F. 2001. School improvement plans in schools on probation: a comparative content analysis across three accountability systems. *Educational Administration Quarterly*, 37(2), 197–218.

Protheroe, N. 2007. What does good math instruction look like? *Principal*, 87(1), 51–54.

First-Order Strategies: The Foundations of Turnaround

When it comes to deciding *how* to improve low-performing schools, planners have hundreds of strategies from which to choose. Strategies can be separated into two basic types. *First-order strategies* constitute the foundations of the turnaround process. They represent schoolwide drivers of change that deal with the overall program of studies and general operational processes. *Second-order strategies* are more specific and focused drivers of change. They address particular problems or issues related to student outcomes. Aligning the curriculum to state standards and standardized tests is a first-order strategy that applies to all core content areas. Double-blocking Algebra 1 for students who struggle with mathematics is a second-order strategy that zeroes in on a particular problem in one content area.

First-order strategies are considered foundational because second-order strategies are unlikely to be very effective unless first-order strategies have been implemented successfully. Double-blocking Algebra 1, for example, is unlikely to benefit students if the Algebra 1 curriculum has not been aligned to the state's end-of-course test that all Algebra students must pass in order to receive academic credit.

There is one other category of actions that should be noted. These actions are not, strictly speaking, strategies, but they play a critical role in the turnaround process. *Facilitators of change* represent the "little things" that principals and teachers do on a daily basis to promote a culture of caring and

KEYS TO SCHOOL TURNAROUND

- First-order strategies: schoolwide drivers of change
- Second-order strategies: focused drivers of change
- Facilitators of change: actions that enable strategies to be implemented successfully

cooperation. These actions range from recognizing when others are working hard to relationship building. It is through these actions that trust and commitment are built. First- and second-order strategies may enable achievement to be raised and gaps to be closed, but facilitators of change increase the odds that these strategies will be implemented successfully.

This chapter addresses first-order strategies, including alignment, instructional focus, teacher teams, scheduling, targeted professional development, student behavior initiatives, family engagement, and faculty building. These drivers of change consistently appear in research on successful school turnarounds (Bryk et al., 2010; Duke et al., 2008; Thompson et al., 2011). It is worth noting, however, that many first-order strategies also can be found in unsuccessful school turnarounds. Alignment can be done well or poorly. So, too, with instructional focus, teacher teams, professional development, and the rest. Success ultimately depends on how well these strategies are implemented and executed on a daily basis.

Bambrick-Santoyo warns turnaround principals to beware of "false drivers" of change. He identifies three in particular. Trying to get complete buy-in from all teachers might sound good, but it can become an unproductive and frustrating distraction. So, too, can overreliance on professional learning communities to direct the turnaround process and an exclusive focus on year-end analysis of assessment data. Bambrick-Santoyo contends that buy-in builds with tangible achievements. As for professional learning communities, he argues that collaboration for the sake of collaboration is not "inherently valuable." Waiting until the end of the year to analyze student achievement is likened to conducting an autopsy. In other words, it comes too late to benefit students. Formative, rather than summative, assessment holds a far greater potential to promote achievement gains (Bambrick-Santoyo, 2010, pp. xxxii–xxxiv).

This chapter's review of first-order strategies is followed by a chapter dealing with specific problems faced by low-performing schools and some second-order strategies for addressing them. Facilitators of change, the "little things" that can have such a great impact on school improvement in general, will be discussed in chapters 7 and 8.

ALIGNMENT

Alignment is complex because the term can be applied to a variety of functions. Resources need to be aligned to planning goals. Professional development ought to be aligned to strategies for school improvement. Energy and effort should be aligned to high-priority initiatives.

Alignment most commonly is applied, however, to the content that students are taught and on which they are tested. It doesn't matter how well teachers are teaching if they are teaching students the wrong content. One of the most serious and widely noted school-based causes of low achievement is the failure of teachers to cover content that students are expected to learn. Turnaround principals must make it their business to find answers to the following questions:

1. Is the content covered in core courses aligned to state standards?
2. Is the content covered in core courses aligned to teacher assessments?
3. Is the content tested in teacher assessments aligned to the content tested in state standardized tests?
4. Are all teachers of the same subject covering the same required content?
5. Is the content covered at one grade level aligned to the content covered in the preceding and the following grade levels? (We refer to this form of alignment as *articulation*.)

Needless to say, determining the answers to these questions and correcting instances of misalignment can require a major investment of time, energy, and resources. It is unlikely, in other words, that correcting widespread misalignment problems can be accomplished in a few months. Turnaround principals may find it helpful to undertake an alignment initiative in stages.

Step 1 might involve a review of the written curriculum, including textbooks, district curriculum documents, written lessons, workbooks, and online content. The objective is to determine the extent to which these written resources reflect state curriculum standards—the standards on which students will be tested. When content misalignment is discovered, principals must see to it that the written curriculum is adjusted. This process has been taking place recently in states that have adopted the Common Core Standards. Still, thorough reviews and revisions of written curriculums are no guarantee that students actually will be taught aligned content.

Step 2 therefore requires a comparison of the revised and aligned written curriculum with the taught curriculum. It probably makes sense to begin this process by focusing on English/language arts and mathematics, since low achievement in these subjects results in schools being singled out for improvement. Determining what teachers actually teach can be challenging, however. Principals and staff members whom they enlist to assist in the process must familiarize themselves with the aligned curriculum and then conduct classroom observations and examinations of student work to determine if students are being taught what they are supposed to be taught.

Once the taught curriculum has been aligned with the written curriculum, the next step involves developing common assessments—the tested curriculum—to be used by all teachers of a particular content area. The purpose of common assessments is to determine how well students are learning required content. These assessments need to be conducted on a regular basis to enable teachers to (1) identify students who are struggling and (2) provide them with timely help. If teachers have to develop their own common assessments—as opposed to purchasing ready-made assessments—considerable time may be required. Work of this kind probably should be undertaken during the summer months when school is not in session.

Turnaround principals may not be able to undertake the foregoing steps as thoroughly as they would like, at least not in the first year or two of the turnaround process. What can be done, however, is to identify the English/language arts and mathematics standards on which students are recording the lowest scores on standardized tests. If there are alignment problems, they are most likely related to these standards. Principals then can call on teachers to focus first on alignment reviews for these standards.

INSTRUCTIONAL FOCUS

Aligning the curriculum naturally leads to the next driver of change—instructional focus. If teachers are teaching the content that students are expected to learn and students continue to struggle, then the next logical place to search for reasons is instruction. Is content not being taught in ways that ensure all students will learn it? The first principals to participate in the University of Virginia's School Turnaround Specialist Program seemed to think so. They identified weak instruction as one of their priority areas for improvement (Duke et.al., 2007).

That instruction is frequently a focus of School Turnaround Plans is hardly surprising. Low-performing schools are rarely able to attract and retain significant numbers of highly qualified teachers. Teacher turnover in these schools is high, and a large percentage of openings are filled by novice teachers.

Focusing on the improvement of instruction is a general strategy that can encompass a variety of components. Low-performing schools, for example, may need to implement Response to Intervention (RtI), an initiative designed to reduce the number of students requiring special education services. RtI consists of three tiers of instruction. The second and third tiers involve small-group and individualized assistance for struggling students, but the first tier—the first line of defense against academic problems—calls for improving the quality of instruction in reading and mathematics for *all* students.

This aspect of RtI makes sense for low-performing schools since a high percentage of students have problems with reading and mathematics. When RtI is first implemented, however, principals should be prepared for large numbers of students to be recommended for Tier II and Tier III services. Making general improvements in instruction based on research may require teachers to learn about and implement differentiated instruction. Flexible classroom routines, varied pacing for students, alternative formats for presenting content, tasks at different levels of difficulty, and student choices are just some of the dimensions of differentiated instruction that have proven useful in low-performing schools (Tomlinson, Brimijoin, and Narvaez, 2008).

Principals can directly and indirectly take a wide array of actions to promote instructional improvement. Some of these efforts are specific to teachers of a particular subject or grade level, while others apply to all teachers. In one study of four principals of Title I schools in North Carolina, principals employed the following strategies to hold teachers accountable for improved instruction:

- One-on-one conversations with teachers on instructional issues
- Clearly articulated expectations regarding work ethic
- Targeted professional development
- Professional Learning Communities
- Regular review of lesson plans
- Frequent classroom visits
- Placement of some teachers on plans of assistance (Corcoran, Peck, and Reitzug, 2013)

When a team of researchers examined principals' efforts to improve instruction in North Carolina's lowest achieving schools, they found some additional strategies that were useful in the turnaround process (Thompson et al., 2011). The development of pacing guides, for example, helped teachers stay on track in their coverage of essential content. Establishing a common format for lesson plans made it easier for teachers of the same subject to compare their lessons and develop aligned assessments. State-supported instructional facilitators also proved useful in providing subject-specific instructional assistance.

One strategy for improving instruction that has received a lot of attention is the classroom walkthrough. Frequent and brief drop-ins are presumed to provide principals (and others) with opportunities to see what teachers are doing and determine if teachers are using sound instructional practices. Like so many other strategies, however, walkthroughs can be done well or poorly. Researchers who collected data on classroom observations by principals in the Miami-Dade School District found, for example, that informal classroom walkthroughs were negatively associated with student achievement (Grissom, Loeb, and Master, 2013). Teachers apparently did not view the walkthroughs as an opportunity for instructional improvement, and principals did not take advantage of these occasions to offer helpful feedback and suggestions.

Some of the best advice for turnaround principals and their faculties can be found in *Why Don't Students Like School?* (Willingham, 2009). In response to the question of how to help "slow learners," Willingham offers a variety of suggestions anchored in cognitive science. Teachers, for example, are urged to praise effort, not ability, and tell students that hard work pays off. Failure should be treated as a natural part of learning rather than an indictment of a student's intelligence. Teachers should not assume that all students understand how to study effectively and efficiently. Study skills, including how to study in groups, need to be taught and reinforced. Instead of always focusing on long-term goals such as catching up with faster-learning peers, teachers should encourage slow learners to work on short-term targets that they can achieve. Doing so helps to boost student confidence. So, too, does showing students that teachers have confidence in their ability to succeed.

Some teachers believe in boosting confidence by giving students easier assignments and less complex content. This approach, when carried too far, ensures that slow learners never catch up with their peers. Turnaround principals must take steps to ensure that all students are exposed to rigorous academic work.

What is involved in rigorous academic work? Instruction needs to move beyond factual content, fluency, and procedural knowledge. Students should focus on problem solving and the application of conceptual knowledge. Activities requiring the synthesis and evaluation of knowledge are important. Students should be expected to raise questions, construct explanations, and defend their explanations. Academic work of this kind is necessary if students are to pass increasingly challenging state tests and go on to tackle post-secondary education.

TEACHER TEAMS

Low-performing schools cannot be turned around by a heroic principal and a few dedicated teachers. The work required to raise student achievement demands a team effort. Developing teams in low-performing schools is not a simple task. Teacher turnover can be high, meaning there are always newcomers to induct and socialize. Low morale and challenging working conditions often present additional obstacles.

Some low-performing schools are like Berkeley Elementary School in rural Virginia—one of the first schools in the University of Virginia School Turnaround Program (Duke et al., 2005). When newly appointed turnaround principal Catherine Thomas arrived in late August, not only did she find no leadership team, teacher committees, or grade-level teams, she confronted a polarized and demoralized faculty. Much of Thomas's early days were spent interviewing teachers to find the leaders she needed to coordinate various teams and form a leadership council.

Nancy Weisskopf encountered a similarly fragmented and toxic situation when she assumed the principalship of South Hills High School in Fort Worth, Texas (Duke and Jacobson, 2011). The school district ordered the faculty to be reconstituted. Only 40 percent of the former faculty could be rehired. Weisskopf therefore faced the challenge of blending together veterans and newcomers. She knew team building would have to begin before school commenced and teachers got caught up in starting their classes. At a retreat in August, she planned to introduce veteran teachers to newcomers. First, however, she met with only the veterans who had been rehired.

Each returning teacher was instructed to write on a piece of paper what they would miss about the old South Hills High School. Then teachers were asked to throw their notes into a fire pit. Weisskopf explained that veteran teachers needed to leave the old South Hills behind when they went into the retreat center to meet their new colleagues. The new South Hills would be nothing like their former school, she told them.

Weisskopf understood that team building could not end when the retreat was over. To be effective, team building needed to be a continuing process. Periodically, Weisskopf scheduled fun team-building activities. On one occasion, for example, she got local businesses to donate bicycle assembly kits and teddy bear sewing kits. She asked her male faculty members to sew together the teddy bears and female faculty members to assemble the bicycles. Getting people out of their comfort zones led to plenty of laughs and bonding. The teddy bears and bicycles were donated to needy children.

Successful turnaround principals like Thomas and Weisskopf know that teams are powerful drivers of change. Teams also can become major impediments to change. Principals must ensure, as Thomas did, that team leaders are positive individuals who support the turnaround process. Individual team members who prevent teams from making progress need to be monitored closely and removed if they refuse to cooperate.

It was not until his third year as turnaround principal of Greer Elementary School in Charlottesville, Virginia, that Matt Landahl felt he had the critical mass of teacher leaders to form teacher-led committees (Duke and Landahl, 2011). By that time he had hired over half the Greer faculty, and he knew the teachers who could be relied upon to move things forward. Committees were set up to address reading improvement, mathematics instruction, scheduling, technology, community relations, and school culture. Greer was well served by these committees and their teacher leaders when Landahl left to take a central office position. Team building and distributed leadership can be a critical element in sustaining successful school turnarounds (Lane, Unger, and Rhim, 2013).

Principals need to determine the team arrangement that best fits the goals of the School Turnaround Plan and the capabilities of the faculty. Elementary schools often have a leadership team, grade-level leaders, and grade-level teams. There also may be vertical teams to ensure curriculum articulation across grade levels and student-assistance teams to identify the needs of struggling students and provide focused help.

Middle schools frequently are organized into instructional teams representing the core subjects of English, social studies, mathematics, and science. Sometimes a special education teacher also is a team member. Each team is responsible for its own group of middle schoolers. There also may be a leadership team, an electives team, and a student-assistance team.

High schools typically have academic departments representing subject matter areas. Some high school principals believe that grade-level teams also can be important in high school. Bringing together all the teachers who work with students at one grade level is invaluable when it comes to identifying struggling students and planning interventions to help them. High schools also have leadership and student-assistance teams.

Principals must never assume that teams are functioning productively. Training in how to organize and operate a team should be provided for team leaders. Team guidelines and protocols can be especially useful. Each team also should have a clear charge from the principal. Some of the functions assigned to teams in turnaround schools include regular review of student-achievement data, discussion of students experiencing academic difficulties, planning interventions to help struggling students, developing common assessments, aligning curriculum, coordinating the school schedule and calendar, planning professional development activities, and developing special programs. To make certain that teams are accomplishing their responsibilities, team leaders should report to principals on a regular basis.

Without an effective team structure, turnaround principals have no option but to hold individuals accountable for raising student achievement. Teams make collective accountability possible. In the most successful turnaround schools, teachers share responsibility for ensuring that all students receive the help they need to succeed. Teams also facilitate the sharing of intellectual capital among teachers. The issues to be confronted in a low-performing school are far too complex for any individual to possess all the answers. By sharing knowledge of students, experience with different strategies, and understanding of local culture, teachers in teams can serve as primary drivers of school turnaround.

SCHEDULING

Time is one of the fundamental resources with which educators have to work. There is a finite amount of time available, and how it is allocated and for what purposes go a long way toward determining student learning. Since many students in low-performing schools have fallen behind their peers in high-performing schools, they are likely to require more instructional time in order to catch up. This also means that their teachers probably require more time to plan lessons, assess progress, and provide assistance.

Principals of successful school turnarounds frequently make adjustments to the daily schedule and sometimes to the yearly calendar as well. These changes may involve increasing the length of the school day; increasing the amount of time allocated for particular subjects; arranging time for teachers to plan together; making greater use of late afternoons, Saturdays, and summers; and expanding the school year. Many of the second-order strategies that you will read about in the next chapter depend upon these adjustments.

Extended school days. Adding time to the school day often is done in order for struggling students to receive timely assistance or for all students to have more time to learn. There is mounting evidence that extended learning time can help raise student achievement (Silva, 2012). Some states even have mandated a longer school day for low-performing schools. Florida, for example, requires its one hundred lowest-performing elementary schools to add an extra hour to the school day and to use that time for reading instruction. Early results suggest the move is paying off (Gewertz, January 22, 2014).

Some turnaround schools operate extensive after-school programs instead of lengthening the official school day. Barcroft Elementary School in Arlington, Virginia, for example, has chosen to offer "specials" such as art, music, and Spanish in its after-school program, thereby allowing teachers to double the time for reading and mathematics during the regular school day.

When after-school time is set aside to help struggling students, it is important to consult parents and students to make certain they support the move. Parents will want to know whether bus transportation is available when their children stay after school to get help. When Nancy Weisskopf asked students at South Hills High School why they were not taking advantage of after-school help, they told her that they were tired of academic work after a full day of school. Some students had after-school jobs or child-care responsibilities. Weisskopf asked them when they preferred to get help. Students suggested one evening a week from 6:00 to 8:00 p.m. Thus began "Monday Madness." Teachers agreed to staff the assistance program, the school district provided transportation, and Weisskopf agreed to buy pizza.

Some extended-day programming relies on volunteers and tutorial services. Principals who draw on such help should monitor it closely. The teachers who know and work with students during the regular school day are likely the best persons to staff extended-day programs. When other individuals are involved, it is important to provide them with training and clear guidelines.

More time for certain subjects. Increasing instructional time in the key subjects of reading/language arts and mathematics is another first-order strategy found in many turnaround schools. The teachers at Greer Elementary School were able to post impressive gains in reading because the principal, Matt Landahl, increased the time for literacy instruction and remediation from 150 to 245 minutes a day (Duke and Landahl, 2011). Decisions of this kind obviously involve trade-offs. Landahl reduced the time allocated to mathematics and social studies instruction.

At the secondary level, some turnaround principals elect to double-block English and Algebra 1 for students who need additional time in these key subjects. The advent of online learning also has made it possible for students to supplement in-class learning with time in a computer lab or on a laptop at home.

Time for teacher planning. Another reason for principals to rethink the school schedule concerns teacher planning time. Teachers appreciate having time to meet and plan during the regular school day instead of staying after school. Building planning time into the regular daily schedule may require considerable creativity on the part of principals, but such actions can pay enormous dividends in terms of teacher support and school reculturing.

Many of the needs for common planning time already have been noted. They include analysis of student-achievement data, curriculum alignment, development of common assessments, and coordination of student assistance. Common planning time also can be used for professional development activities.

Afternoons, Saturdays, and summers. Additional learning time can be found by looking beyond the conventional hours of school (Bodilly et al. 2010). In some school districts, students who have fallen behind in the accumulation of graduation credits attend late afternoon or evening classes in order to make up credits. Summers provide an additional opportunity for credit recovery as well as academic assistance and enrichment (Augustine et al., 2013).

Another reason for low-performing schools to run summer programs concerns loss of learning (Augustine et al., 2013). Students from well-to-do homes are less likely to experience loss of learning over the summer than students from less affluent homes. Researchers, in fact, have traced the achievement gap between high- and low-SES ninth graders to differences in summer learning during the elementary years (Alexander, Entwisle, and Olson, 2007). Students from low-SES homes typically lack the opportunities to travel and participate in extra learning experiences that their more well-to-do peers enjoy. Teachers in low-performing schools complain that valuable time at the beginning of each school year must be spent reteaching material from the previous year. Summer programs can help to supplement student learning and reduce the time needed to review previously taught material.

Some schools take advantage of Saturdays to increase instructional time and enable students to make up missing assignments. Other schools schedule special Saturday review sessions before students take standardized tests in the spring.

Principals who intend to supplement learning by arranging late afternoon, evening, Saturday, and summer programs are advised to plan ahead, choose instructors carefully, and provide training for instructors. Some of these supplementary programs may be run in conjunction with community agencies and cultural institutions. The key to success, as in so many areas of school turnaround, is focus. Trying to accomplish too many purposes in one program can result in disappointing outcomes.

Expanded calendar. Sometimes lengthening the school day still does not provide enough additional time to meet the needs of students. Under such circumstances, lengthening the school year may be warranted. This situation faced Mel Riddile when he became principal of Stuart High School in Fairfax County, Virginia.

Stuart was a low-performing high school that enrolled a large percentage of English language learners. To meet the needs of these students, Riddile reorganized Stuart into three units. Students who spoke no English were assigned to a self-contained class where the primary focus was learning English. When these students acquired adequate English to study other subjects, they were transferred to a team of teachers who helped them acquire background knowledge in core subjects. Once they demonstrated an understanding of the knowledge that middle schoolers were supposed to have acquired, students moved into regular high school classes.

This process often took a year or more. As a result, students fell behind in earning the credits needed to graduate on time from high school. Riddile realized that the school year had to be expanded in order for many Stuart students to make up credits. It took him several years of gaining the support of parents and teachers, district authorities, and finally the state Board of Education, but Riddile persisted and eventually was allowed to run courses on a year-round basis. By the time Riddile left, Stuart had become a model of high school turnaround (Duke, 2010).

Lengthening the school day and school year obviously entail additional expenditures. A team of researchers examined what it cost for five schools to expand learning time (Kaplan et al., 2014). The annual additional hours ranged from 132 to 540 hours. The extra time was used for a variety of purposes, including daily intervention blocks, additional class time, enrichment classes, daily tutoring, collaborative planning, and professional development. The additional per pupil cost per hour ranged from $2.20 to $5.23. Funds were obtained from federal, state, district, and philanthropic sources.

Increasing instructional time has the potential to contribute to school turnaround, but it is not a panacea. If strategies to improve instruction are not paired with expanded learning time, the likelihood of achievement gains is slight. Greater exposure to mediocre instruction is hardly a step in the right direction.

PROFESSIONAL DEVELOPMENT

Because instruction in low-performing schools, almost by definition, is inadequate, professional development is the only strategy other than replacing teachers that can produce the instructional improvements necessary to drive school turnaround. There are, of course, other reasons besides instructional improvement for professional development. Teachers also may need to learn about new assessments, data-driven decision making, Common Core Standards, Professional Learning Communities, innovative technology, and programs designed to reduce disorder and misconduct.

Once again, focus is the key. Professional development that is not aligned to specific objectives in the School Turnaround Plan and that does not focus on the skills and knowledge needed to implement particular strategies is unlikely to result in substantive gains. Sadly, many educators have experienced the frustration of attending workshops and training sessions that contribute little to their immediate needs.

How professional development is delivered can be as important as what it focuses on. One-shot workshops, for example, rarely have much of an effect. Elsewhere, I have offered some cautionary advice regarding professional development:

- Don't assume that a single exposure to new knowledge is sufficient.
- Don't assume that new knowledge automatically displaces old knowledge.
- Don't assume that people change without feedback.
- Don't assume that the source of feedback is unimportant.
- Don't assume that novices and veterans learn in identical ways. (Duke, 2004, p. 149)

In planning professional development, turnaround principals need to sustain exposure to new methods and material so that faculty members have an opportunity to practice using them. As noted in chapter 1, old ways of doing things must be shown to be ineffective before many individuals will embrace new ways. This takes time and lots of feedback. The source of this feedback is significant. Sometimes the best source of feedback is another teacher or outside expert, not the principal. When trust has been established between teachers and principals, however, principals also can be effective sources of feedback.

New teachers frequently are more receptive to feedback aimed at improving their practice than veteran teachers. Principals therefore may need to differentiate professional development. New teachers, for example, may respond well to professional development activities involving their colleagues. Veteran teachers, on the other hand, may find individual coaching to be less threatening.

One benefit of coaching is that guidance can be provided in the classroom as lessons actually are being conducted. Coaches have an opportunity to observe students as well as instruction and tailor their advice to the specific context in which a teacher is teaching. Low-performing schools often have access to literacy and math coaches along with instructional specialists. Many turnaround principals find that coaching is an effective follow-up to staff training. Coaches can reinforce what teachers learned in the training and offer support when difficulties are encountered.

It is important for principals to attend professional development activities that are intended for the entire faculty. Their presence signals the importance of the activities and enables them to understand what teachers are expected to learn. During routine walkthroughs and observations, principals then can check to see whether new practices are being applied.

Lesson Study is a professional development model that has attracted considerable attention in recent years. One form of Lesson Study involves a teacher presenting a lesson from one of their classes to fellow teachers, who then offer feedback regarding the design of the lesson and how it might be delivered more effectively. Another form of Lesson Study calls on a group of teachers to design a lesson from scratch and then pilot test it. Following the pilot test, the teachers meet to critique and fine-tune the lesson.

When considering professional development as a school turnaround strategy, principals should not forget their own leadership team. Researchers studying turnarounds in North Carolina found that members of leadership teams felt timely training on how to develop Action Plans and align curriculum, instruction, and assessment were particularly valuable (Thompson et al., 2011). Principals themselves also can benefit from professional development as they undertake the challenges of the turnaround process. Where coaches or mentors are not provided for principals by the school district or state education department, turnaround principals may want to secure such services on their own.

Turnaround Tip: Principals of low-performing schools can benefit from having their own coach or mentor.

STRATEGIES ADDRESSING STUDENT BEHAVIOR

The likelihood of raising student achievement in a school characterized by disorder is slight. Teachers in low-performing schools frequently complain that too much instructional time is devoted to dealing with behavior problems in class. Bullying, harassment, and fighting can cause many students to fear for their safety. Identifying strategies that promote safe and orderly classrooms and corridors is one of the first orders of business for many turnaround principals (Bryk et al., 2010; Duke et al., 2007; Thompson et al., 2011).

Student behavior problems are so varied that one strategy is unlikely to be sufficient. A strategy aimed at reducing fighting in the hallways may not help curtail classroom disruptions. Strategies that work in elementary schools may not be appropriate for secondary schools.

In considering which strategies best address particular disciplinary concerns, you may find it helpful to distinguish between intervention, prevention, and management strategies (Duke, 2002).

Intervention strategies are intended to deal effectively with behavior problems and threats to school safety that actually are occurring. The objective is to minimize the impact of these incidents and reduce the likelihood that they recur. Frequently used intervention strategies include counseling, behavior modification, parental contact, peer mediation, student reassignment or placement in an alternative setting, and, of course, punishment. The impact of these strategies is often debated. Inconsistent application of strategies and strategies that are perceived by students to be discriminatory can undermine effectiveness.

Strategies involving restorative practices have the potential to improve relations between educators and students while simultaneously serving as effective interventions (Mirsky and Korr, 2014). Restorative practices involve post-incident meetings between students and staff members. Meetings provide opportunities to explore what happened, hold the student accountable for the incident, and repair the harm. The process enables the student to learn how their actions affected others. If the student has to be suspended, a similar meeting should be held when the student returns to school.

Prevention strategies derive from an understanding of the root causes of behavior problems. The objective is to eliminate the conditions that give rise to problems, thereby reducing the need for intervention. School rules are an obvious example of a prevention strategy. Principals hope that punishments for violating rules will serve as deterrents, and for many students this is the case. Other students break the rules and are punished, the hope being that they will not repeat the offense.

If the cause of misbehavior derives from frustration associated with lack of academic success, prevention strategies must involve instructional adjustments. Efforts to improve classroom climate and school culture, dress codes, and initiatives that recognize and reward students for good behavior represent popular approaches to preventing behavior problems from occurring in the first place.

Some approaches to prevention actually are comprehensive programs involving a variety of strategies. Two of the most widely used programs are Responsive Classroom and Positive Behavioral Interventions and Supports (PBIS). The latter is designed to alter the school environment by implementing improved systems of discipline, positive reinforcement, and data management (Barrett, Bradshaw, and Lewis-Palmer, 2008; Thompson et al., 2011). Responsive Classroom emphasizes emotional support for students, positive teacher-student relations, and daily opportunities for students to discuss their concerns and address classroom issues.

Management strategies are an acknowledgement that some behavior problems and threats to safety are likely to occur despite the presence of prevention programs and interventions. Management strategies focus on handling problems in ways that minimize their adverse effects on teaching and learning. Crisis management plans, required for most schools, are an example of a management strategy. So, too, are specialized personnel, such as deans of students, school resource officers, and crisis counselors.

FAMILY ENGAGEMENT

Enlisting the support of parents and other relatives in the school turnaround process can be one of the most important first-order strategies. Having noted this, it also should be pointed out that parent involvement can be one of the most challenging and frustrating strategies to implement. Low-performing schools often are located in poor neighborhoods where the difficulties of daily life present impediments to parent involvement in schools.

One program that has succeeded in engaging parents and other community members is the School Development Program created by James Comer (2004). Designed to focus on improving the social climate among adults in schools, the program's work is accomplished by three teams: a parent team, a planning and management team, and a student and staff support team. All three teams are expected to follow three basic principles. First, team efforts should focus on problem solving, not fixing blame. Second, team decisions should avoid creating winners and losers. Third, collaboration rather than competition should characterize the work among stakeholder groups.

When Charles Payne (2008) observed Comer's program at work in Chicago schools where parent involvement previously had been rare, he found that participation soared after introduction of the program. According to Payne, parents "were patrolling hallways and playgrounds, acting as classroom aides, doing lunchroom duties, and in some cases even taking over classes while teachers did professional development" (p. 202). Children felt good about having parents around, and parents felt pride about participating in their children's education. Some volunteers even were able to secure paying jobs as a result of their involvement. Teachers who previously regarded some parents as adversaries and critics developed an appreciation for them and their commitment to supporting the school.

The findings of a longitudinal study of Chicago elementary schools extends Payne's observations, noting that school turnaround efforts may need to reach beyond school walls into poor neighborhoods in order to cultivate local leadership and build connections to local service agencies (Bryk et al., 2010). The social, emotional, and health needs of young people out of school as well as in school cannot be overlooked, the researchers conclude, if academic achievement is to be raised.

Principals alone cannot increase parent and community engagement. Making a point of identifying influential local leaders early in the turnaround process can pay enormous dividends down the road. These individuals can arrange opportunities for principals and staff members to meet parents and other community members. Such meetings serve to build trust and open channels of communication between home and school. Some principals hire an individual to serve as a coordinator of community outreach efforts.

Involving parents in developing School Turnaround Plans already has been noted as an important way to build trust. Appointing one or two parents to a School Improvement Team, however, is not a substitute for broad-based participation. In some cases, such participation will depend on scheduling meetings outside of regular school hours and in locations convenient to parents.

BUILDING A CAPABLE FACULTY

More than any other factor, the strategies that principals of low-performing schools employ to build a competent and cohesive faculty have the potential to make the greatest impact on student learning and well-being. When it comes to personnel matters, however, principals are not always able to act on their own. Decisions regarding who to hire and who to let go may be governed by contracts, legalities, government mandates, and district policies.

Low-performing schools that receive federal school improvement funds and choose the so-called "turnaround option," for example, must reconstitute the faculty. Requiring faculty members to reapply for their jobs and rehiring only a portion of them is a controversial policy, especially for schools that have trouble recruiting and retaining teachers in the first place. There is some evidence, though, that this dramatic action can yield benefits. A study of Level 4 schools in Massachusetts found that eight of nine schools that made significant gains in achievement replaced at least 50 percent of their teachers in the first year of the state-mandated turnaround process (Lane, Unger, and Rhim, 2013). All nine of the Level 4 schools that made no gains in achievement retained 65 percent or more of their faculty. Similar positive results for replacing large numbers of teachers were found by a team of researchers studying turnaround efforts in North Carolina's lowest achieving schools (Thompson et al., 2011).

Collective bargaining contracts also can constrain principals when it comes to building a capable faculty. Contracts often protect teachers with seniority, even when their performance falls short of less senior teachers. Teacher unions in some locations, however, have been willing to set aside seniority rules for chronically low-performing schools, thereby freeing principals to retain teachers with the best track records for teaching struggling students.

Principals of low-performing schools have three major responsibilities when it comes to building a capable faculty. As Jim Collins (2001) would say, their first duty is to see that they have the right people on the bus. Next, they need to make certain that their riders are in the right seats. After ensuring that the faculty consists of capable teachers who are placed in positions where they can make the greatest contribution to student learning, principals finally must create working conditions that lead to high rates of teacher retention.

Principals who are unable to launch the turnaround process by hiring a substantial number of new teachers need to focus initially on analyzing achievement data, conducting observations of teachers, and determining which teachers are not effective. These teachers then must be provided with unambiguous feedback on the areas where they need to improve and a timeline for improvement. In the most serious cases, teachers will have to be put on a formal plan of assistance. Confronting ineffective teachers demands a measure of courage on the principal's part. Donaldson (2013) discovered that principals sometimes admit to scaling back efforts to increase teacher effectiveness in order to preserve congenial relations with the faculty. Placing teacher relations ahead of student learning, however, is unacceptable for principals of low-performing schools, or any schools for that matter.

In some cases, a teacher's lack of effectiveness may be a function of placement rather than proficiency. Recognizing that some elementary teachers may not be equally effective teaching reading and mathematics, for instance, principals can move to a departmentalized staffing model (also known as *platooning*) (Gewertz, February 19, 2014). Students work on reading and literacy with one teacher, then go to another teacher for math instruction.

It is also the case that some teachers may be better equipped to provide intensive assistance to individuals and small groups of students than to handle large-group instruction. Principals should devote considerable time to assessing teachers' strengths and weaknesses and then assigning teachers in ways that take advantage of their talents.

Every school, no matter how poor its performance, has some teachers who are more effective than others. A unique study using four years' worth of achievement data for fifth and eighth grade teachers in North Carolina found that identifying a school's most effective teachers can pay dividends, at least at the eighth grade level (Hansen, 2013). Using a sophisticated statistical simulation, the researcher concluded that assigning up to twelve more students to a school's most effective eighth grade teachers can produce impressive achievement gains—gains equivalent to adding two-and-a-half weeks of instruction!

It is the custom in some schools for highly qualified teachers to be assigned to teach high-achieving students. Principals must consider the costs and benefits of perpetuating this custom. In the medical community, the most challenging cases often are referred to the most highly regarded specialists. Principals of low-performing schools need to find ways to expose struggling students to the best teaching talent available.

Some faculty-building strategies call for adding teachers and specialists to faculty ranks. Low-performing high schools, for example, may find that adding a reading specialist to the faculty can be a valuable source of assistance for students who continue to struggle with comprehending text. Other strategies may call for pairing teachers to increase their impact on student learning. Such arrangements sometimes involve tandems consisting of a content specialist and either a special education or an English as a Second Language teacher. Another staffing strategy involves one teacher continuing to teach the same group of students for two or more years. *Looping*, as this arrangement is called, can provide students with consistent care, concern, and instruction, reducing the possible disruptive effects of switching teachers every year.

When Nancy Weisskopf became principal of South Hills High School, she brought a former football coach on board to do nothing but maintain contact with students who were falling behind in their school work. Relying on his popularity with students and his unique talent for showing that he cared about their welfare, this individual met regularly with students to make sure they sought help when they needed it and completed assignments. When students missed school, he made home visits to ensure they were all right.

Turnaround principals also may want to consider hiring an administrative assistant or school manager to handle routine administrative duties, thereby freeing up their time for instructional leadership. When principals get caught up in managerial tasks and lose touch with teachers and what's going on in classrooms, the focus on improving achievement can easily be lost. The point has been made before: the primary responsibility of a school leader is leading. Staffing the school office in ways that allow the principal to lead is critical to the success of turnaround efforts.

―∞―

Turnaround Tip: The school office should be staffed for handling managerial duties so that the principal can focus on instructional leadership.

―∞―

Besides hiring capable teachers and seeing that they are properly placed, principals of low-performing schools should take steps to ensure that effective teachers remain on the faculty. Reducing teacher turnover is an important key to sustaining school improvement. Strategies to increase retention will be addressed later in the book.

Many first-order strategies have been presented in this chapter. Principals of low-performing schools may be tempted to try and implement lots of them in their first 90-day plan. To do so would be a mistake. Focus remains the guiding principle. Choosing a few strategies to implement increases the chances of success. As is so often the case, success is likely to breed success, or at least it is more likely to breed success than failure to implement strategies because too many strategies were undertaken at one time.

―∞―

Turnaround Tip: Principals should resist the temptation to implement too many first-order strategies at one time.

―∞―

Principals need to carefully assess their school's circumstances, including student concerns, available resources, and teacher strengths and weaknesses. Ultimately, a judgment will have to be made regarding which first-order strategies are mostly likely to be implemented successfully, thereby laying the groundwork for tackling additional strategies.

REFERENCES

Alexander, K. L.; Entwisle, D. R.; and Olson, L. S. 2007. Lasting consequences of the summer learning gap. *American Sociological Review*, 72(3), 167–180.

Augustine, C. H.; McCombs, J. S.; Schwartz, H. L.; and Zakaras, L. 2013. Getting to work on summer learning. Santa Monica, CA: RAND.

Bambrick-Santoyo, P. 2010. *Driven by Data*. San Francisco: Jossey-Bass.

Barrett, S. B.; Bradshaw, C. P.; and Lewis-Palmer, T. 2008. Maryland statewide PBIS initiative. *Journal of Positive Behavior Interventions,* 10(2), 105–114.

Bodilly, S. J.; McCombs, J. S.; Orr, N.; Scherer, E.; Constant, L.; and Gershwin, D. 2010. *Hours of Opportunity,* Vol. 1. Santa Monica, CA: RAND.

Bryk, A. S.; Sebring, P. B.; Allensworth, E.; Luppescu, S.; and Easton, J. Q. 2010. *Organizing Schools for Improvement.* Chicago: University of Chicago Press.

Collins, J. 2001. *Good to Great.* New York: Harper Business.

Comer, J. P. 2004. *Leave No Child Behind.* New Haven, CT: Yale University Press.

Corcoran, C.; Peck, C.; and Reitzug, U. C. 2013. Exiting school improvement sanctions. In B. Barnett, A. R. Shoho, and A. J. Bowers (eds.), *School and District Leadership in an Era of Accountability.* Charlotte, NC: Information Age Publishing (IAP), 63–83.

Donaldson, M. L. 2013. Principals' approaches to cultivating teacher effectiveness: constraints and opportunities in hiring, assigning, evaluating, and developing teachers. *Educational Administration Quarterly,* 49(5), 838–882.

Duke, D. L. 2004. *The Challenges of Educational Change.* Boston: Pearson.

Duke, D. L. 2002. *Creating Safe Schools for All Children.* Boston: Allyn & Bacon.

Duke, D. L. 2010. *Differentiating School Leadership.* Thousand Oaks, CA: Corwin.

Duke, D. L. and Jacobson, M. 2011. Tackling the toughest turnaround—low-performing high schools. *Kappan,* 92(5), 34–38.

Duke, D. L. and Landahl, M. 2011. "Raising test scores was the easy part": A case study of the third year of school turnaround. *International Studies in Educational Administration,* 39(3), 91–114.

Duke, D. L.; Tucker, P. D.; Belcher, M.; Crews, D.; Harrison-Coleman, J.; Higgins, J.; Lanphear, L.; Marshall, M.; Reasor, H.; Richardson, S.; Rose, M.; Salmonowicz, M. J.; Scott, W.; Taylor, R.; Thomas, C.; and West, J. 2005. *Lift-Off: Launching the School Turnaround Process in Ten Virginia Schools.* Charlottesville, VA: Partnership for Leaders in Education, University of Virginia.

Duke, D. L.; Tucker, P. D.; Salmonowicz, M. J.; and Levy, M. 2007. How comparable are the perceived challenges facing principals of low-performing schools? *International Studies in Educational Administration,* 35(1), 3–21.

Duke, D. L.; Tucker, P. D.; Salmonowicz, M. J.; Levy, M.; and Saunders, S. 2008. *Teachers' Guide to School Turnarounds.* Lanham, MD: Rowman & Littlefield.

Gewertz, C. January 22, 2014. Fla. pushes longer day with more reading in struggling schools. *Education Week,* 33(18), 1, 12.

Gewertz, C. February 19, 2014. "Platooning" on rise in early grades. *Education Week,* 33(21), 1, 16–17.

Grissom, J. A.; Loeb, S.; and Master, B. 2013. Effective instructional time use for school leaders: longitudinal evidence from observations of principals. *Educational Researcher,* 42(8), 433–444.

Hansen, M. 2013. Right-sizing the classroom: Making the most of great teachers. Washington, DC: Thomas B. Fordham Institute.

Kaplan, C.; Farbman, D. A.; Deich, S.; and Padgette, H. C. 2014. *Financing Expanded Learning Time in Schools.* Boston, MA: National Center on Time & Learning.

Lane, B.; Unger, C.; and Rhim, L. M. 2013. *Emerging and Sustaining Practices for School Turnaround.* Baltimore, MD: Institute for Strategic Leadership and Learning.

Mirsky, L. and Korr, S. 2014. Restoring community and trust. *Principal Leadership,* 14(6), 32–35.

Payne, C. M. 2008. *So Much Reform, So Little Change.* Cambridge, MA: Harvard Education Press.

Silva, E. 2012. *Off the Clock: What More Time Can (and Can't) Do for School Turnarounds.* Washington, DC: Education Sector.

Thompson, C. L.; Brown, K. M.; Townsend, L. W.; Henry, G. T.; and Fortner, C. K. 2011. *Turning Around North Carolina's Lowest Achieving Schools (2006–2010).* Chapel Hill, NC: Consortium for Educational Research and Evaluation—North Carolina.

Tomlinson, C. A.; Brimijoin, K.; and Narvaez, L. 2008. *The Differentiated School.* Alexandria, VA: Association for Supervision and Curriculum Development (ASCD).

Willingham, D. T. 2009. *Why Don't Students Like School?* San Francisco: Jossey-Bass.

Second-Order Strategies: Getting Focused on Student Outcomes

The preceding chapter provided examples of how first-order strategies create the conditions needed to support focused efforts to address student outcomes. Without these conditions, strategies aimed at eliminating the impediments to improved achievement are unlikely to succeed. A great many of the second-order strategies presented in this chapter concern delivering help to students, both individually and collectively. Without help that goes above and beyond normal instructional interactions, many students in low-performing schools will continue to fall further and further behind.

Chapter 6 is organized into sections dealing with the kinds of challenges facing low-performing schools. Each section offers examples of second-order strategies that are designed to address a particular challenge. There are far more strategies than can be discussed in one chapter, but the examples illustrate what can be done to address some of the more common goals and objectives of School Turnaround Plans.

The chapter begins by looking at the issue of student absenteeism. Subsequent sections discuss poor work habits, reading problems at the high school level, the needs of English language learners, student transition to ninth grade, and high school dropouts. Some second-order strategies can be applied to a number of these challenges. Others are appropriate for only one challenge. Much of the work of developing School Turnaround Plans involves deciding which second-order strategies are most likely to address the causes of specific challenges.

ABSENTEEISM

The point is obvious. Students who are not in class are less likely to learn what they need to learn in order to progress in school and eventually graduate. Students miss class and are absent from school for a variety of reasons, so any plan that attempts to reduce absenteeism should be based on an understanding of these causes. Causes include fear of bullying, negative peer pressure, poor instruction, feelings of hopelessness, chronic illness, hurtful relations with teachers, lack of preparation for class, and commitments outside of school. Strategies that address one cause may not necessarily be appropriate for another cause.

Insight into the causes of absenteeism can be gained by analyzing attendance data. Are there patterns to student absenteeism? Are students more likely to miss the first class of the day? If so, it could indicate problems with oversleeping or transportation to school. Does the rate of class cutting spike after lunch? If so, are students leaving school or just lingering with friends? Is absenteeism higher on certain days of the week or during certain times of the year?

When newly appointed turnaround principal J. Harrison-Coleman analyzed tardiness data, she discovered that many students got to her elementary school on time every day but Friday. Her second-order strategy involved organizing a fun preschool activity every Friday. A loudspeaker in front of school blaring popular music announced "Dancing into Friday" to the nearby housing project from which her students came. Parents, students, teachers, staff members, and administrators started each Friday dancing together. Not only did these events reduce tardiness, but they also helped build community spirit.

Relying on punishments to reduce chronic absenteeism generally has not proven effective in low-performing schools. What good does it do, for example, to suspend a chronic truant? Doing so may actually be perceived by the student as a reward! Doubts also have been raised about the value of in-school suspension. Automatically suspending students who miss too much school fails to take into account the reasons why they are frequently absent.

Depending on the reason why some students cut class and miss school, the following strategies may be effective:

- Academic assistance programs
- Social support
- Anti-bullying initiatives
- Community agency involvement

- Parent cooperation
- Alternative education

Academic assistance. Students who frequently are absent because they are not prepared for class or are failing to keep up with classmates require targeted assistance. Rather than assigning students to a yearlong study hall or after-school program, assistance is best provided on an as-needed basis. Keeping up with out-of-class assignments can be difficult for students whose living situations are unsettled. It is important that these students not be allowed to fall so far behind in their school work that they feel it is hopeless to try and catch up.

At South Hills High School, principal Nancy Weisskopf initiated "Just Do It" days to make certain that students did not fall behind. When teachers reported that a student was not turning in assignments, Weisskopf dispatched one of her assistant principals to pull the student out of first period class without prior notice. The student was taken to a quiet room for the entire day and instructed to complete missing assignments. One "Just Do It" day typically was sufficient to curtail the problem of missed assignments.

Social support. Absenteeism also can result from feeling like one does not belong. Such feelings sometimes arise when students move from one school to another or when they have to repeat a grade. The best form of social support is a caring relationship with a teacher, staff member, or peer. Such relationships do not always require a formalized program or strategy. Where significant numbers of students feel disconnected, however, a peer mentoring program or teacher advisory program may be warranted. School authorities also can work with community groups like Big Brothers and Big Sisters to arrange for social support by community members.

There are no shortcuts to building relationships. If such connections between teachers and students are important—and of course they are—it is vital for principals to see that teachers' time is not filled up with less important responsibilities. Extracurricular activities often provide effective avenues for relationship building. Encouraging students in low-performing schools to get involved in sports, musical activities, school plays, and clubs increases the opportunities for students and teachers to get to know each other.

Anti-bullying initiatives. One of the most frequently mentioned reasons for missing school is concern for personal safety. Tragic consequences can result when students are bullied, harassed, and hazed by other students. Anti-bullying initiatives typically begin by raising awareness of the problem. Students are encouraged to discuss their safety concerns with counselors and teachers as well as in small groups of peers who share similar concerns. The website stopbullying. gov (http://www.stopbullying.gov/) recommends that efforts to reduce bullying should involve parents as well as students and school staff. If a school does not have a policy regarding bullying and specific rules and consequences associated with such behavior, the principal needs to see that they are developed and shared with the school community.

The next step involves establishing a system by which students can safely report acts of bullying. Educating students and staff members about how to handle bullying also is important. In the long run, however, creating a school culture of respect, caring, and acceptance of differences stands the best chance of reducing bullying.

Agency involvement. In some cases where absenteeism persists and parents refuse to cooperate with school authorities, principals may need to involve outside agencies or even the court system. It is a good idea for principals to establish links with local social service and law enforcement agencies, even if absenteeism is not currently a serious issue. Then, if problems do arise, principals know who to contact and what assistance can be provided.

Local police may be willing to help by picking up students who are truant. Large school systems sometimes employ truant officers and establish truancy centers to which truant students can be taken when they are picked up. If students are habitually truant, it may be necessary to take them and their parents or guardians to court. Before resorting to such drastic measures, however, principals must see to it that students, parents, and guardians understand what the school is prepared to do to reduce truancy. These parties should be informed about what does and does not constitute an "excused" absence.

Parent cooperation. Significant headway in efforts to reduce absenteeism is unlikely to be made without the cooperation of parents and guardians. School personnel should make parents aware of the possible consequences of missing too many days of school. One study cited in chapter 3 found that students who missed at least 20 percent of school days in the sixth grade had a 75 percent chance of dropping out of high school. Truancy also is a predictor of delinquency (*Improving School Attendance*, 2005). Enlisting parent assistance as soon as a student begins to exhibit attendance problems should be a fundamental component of any program intended to reduce truancy.

Initiatives designed to reduce truancy cannot begin too early in a child's schooling. When student absenteeism began to rise in Richmond, Virginia, an all-out effort was made at the elementary school level to nip the problem in the bud. Special teams at elementary schools met with parents of children who missed six or more days of school. Home visits were made when any student missed more than ten days of school. Intervening to reduce absenteeism by young students eventually paid dividends by reducing the dropout rate in Richmond (Diplomas Count, 2013).

A system for notifying parents and guardians when their children are absent from school or missing class needs to be set up if one does not already exist. It is also helpful when parents take the initiative to inform the school office when their children will not be in school. This is especially important when children are reluctant to go to school because of bullying and problems with teachers. Maintaining regular contact with parents and guardians becomes more challenging as children grow older, but keeping lines of communication open in middle and high school is essential if absenteeism is to be kept to a minimum.

Alternative education. Despite the best efforts of parents and educators, some students may continue to miss too many days of school. In these cases placement in an alternative program should be considered. Alternative programs range from special in-school programs to small schools occupying separate facilities. Alternative programs accommodate the special needs of their students, such as modified daily schedules for students with child-care responsibilities and jobs. Some alternative programs make extensive use of individualized and computer-based instruction. A key feature of these programs is their small size and emphasis on close, supportive relationships with students.

Principals of low-performing schools who see a need for an in-school alternative program should realize that it will take time to set up and staff the program. How students are assigned to an alternative program needs to be specified along with expectations for attendance, behavior, and academic progress. Alternative programs in many cases are a last resort before students drop out of school.

POOR WORK HABITS

Educators are well aware of the fact that academic success depends on students acquiring a variety of cognitive skills. Students must learn to comprehend written material, discriminate among seemingly similar phenomena, generalize, evaluate, and so on. Research has shown that students also need to develop various work habits and dispositions in order to achieve academic success (Tough, 2012). These habits and dispositions sometimes are referred to as *noncognitive skills*, though this term may be a misnomer.

Work habits and dispositions ideally develop early in life, often before young people begin school. Learning to deal with disappointment and frustration, knowing how to handle new challenges, and understanding the relationship between effort and achievement are some of the keys to success in school and beyond. Unfortunately, some young people, particularly those raised in poverty and dysfunctional homes, may not have developed these attributes at an early age. Under such circumstances, it is up to educators to fill in the gaps.

Among the strategies that have proven helpful in cultivating constructive habits and dispositions in students are the following:

- Direct instruction concerning intelligence and learning
- Reinforcing the value of effort and academic work
- Teaching perseverance
- Developing self-efficacy
- Stressing self-regulation

Direct instruction. Educators should not assume that students understand how intelligence and learning actually work. Many people, including adults, consider intelligence, for example, to be a fixed trait, one that is unlikely to change because of instruction. When students in low-performing schools believe that they are less intelligent than other students and that intelligence is fixed, they are less likely to invest hope and energy in their schooling. Sadly, they even may accept the stereotype that kids in low-performing schools are not capable of high-level learning (Steele, 2010).

The fact is that intelligence is *not* a fixed trait (Farrington et al., 2012). Strategies have been found that help young people understand that they can become high-level learners. One strategy involves providing students with direct instruction regarding intelligence and how it can change as a result of focus and effort (Farrington et al., 2012). Such instruction may best be provided outside of class, perhaps in an advisory group.

Teachers should take every opportunity to tell students that they belong in an academic environment and that they are capable of achieving at high levels. Such reminders, of course, must be reinforced by actions. Teachers, for example, must not reserve challenging questions and assignments only for a select group of students.

Reinforcing the value of effort and academic work. Instruction is not the only way that teachers can have an impact on students. Casual comments and informal conversations also influence what students do and how they feel about themselves and their schooling. Teachers should take every opportunity to stress the importance of effort and academic work. Students need to believe that they can succeed when they apply themselves and that doing so leads to worthwhile outcomes.

Encouraging students to project into the future and anticipate how what they are doing in school can lead to desired results has been shown to be an effective strategy (Farrington et al., 2012). So, too, has getting students to set short-range goals (Willingham, 2009). Achieving these goals provides teachers with opportunities to praise student effort and increases the odds students will undertake additional goals. A third strategy involves having students write about how the topics they are studying can be applied to their own lives (Hulleman and Harackiewicz, 2009). Students who did so in ninth grade science classes saw sizeable improvements in their grades.

Teachers should never assume that students can make connections between course content and the knowledge they will need to succeed in life. Exposing students to adult role models who can explain how their studies in school benefitted them later in life helps young people begin to make these connections. Since students who grow up in poor neighborhoods may be unaware of the variety of occupations available to adults, teachers should provide examples of careers that require the knowledge that they are helping students acquire.

Teaching perseverance. Criticism of young people today often notes their seeming unwillingness to delay gratification or persist when they encounter challenging content. Educators sometimes enable this behavior by allowing students to quit when at first they don't succeed or by giving them easier assignments.

Some research suggests that teaching students about the importance of perseverance can lead to greater willingness to persist with challenging work (Farrington et al., 2012). Other researchers call on teachers to present challenging work in ways that make success seem attainable (Dweck, Walton, and Cohen, 2011). Whatever strategy is employed, teachers need to provide continuing support and encouragement when students tackle difficult tasks.

Developing self-efficacy. Self-efficacy is the belief that one is able to undertake the actions necessary to accomplish desired objectives (Bandura, 1997). Individuals with a weak sense of self-efficacy avoid challenging tasks, lack confidence, and dwell on personal failings. These characteristics undermine student success in school and lead to hopelessness, alienation, and dropping out of school.

Teachers have a vital role to play in developing and reinforcing self-efficacy. Since the most effective way of cultivating a strong sense of self-efficacy is through mastery experiences, teachers can structure difficult assignments by using a series of manageable steps or tasks. If students get stuck at any point along the road to mastery, teachers can model what needs to be done. These strategies have proven effective for younger and older students alike, and special education classrooms often employ them. The confidence that comes from reaching mastery on one objective frequently provides the impetus needed to tackle other objectives.

Stressing self-regulation. To be self-regulated is "to be goal-directed and to demonstrate control over and responsibility for one's focus and effort when engaged in a learning activity" (Le and Wolfe, 2013, p. 37). Self-regulation does not come naturally; it must be learned. Like self-efficacy, self-regulation can be modeled. It is important for teachers to create an expectation that students will become self-regulating.

One strategy associated with the development of self-regulation involves student-led conferences. Instead of having teachers conduct end-of-grading-period conferences to report student progress to parents, students assume responsibility for planning and conducting conferences. Teachers and parents listen as students explain how they are doing in the class, share work samples, and discuss areas where they are having difficulty. Students who become accustomed to conducting these conferences do not have to rely on teachers to tell them where they stand in class.

Another dimension of self-regulation involves knowing when to ask and how to ask for help. Teachers should work with students to develop ways for them to obtain assistance that are not embarrassing. Finding time to meet with students individually is important. So, too, is designating a secure website as a way to receive help.

Teachers who provide students with opportunities to conduct self-assessments reinforce the importance of self-regulation (Stiggins, 2005). To prepare students to self-assess, teachers need to instruct students on what to look for in order to determine how well they are doing with particular content and assignments. Actual examples of assignments that have been done well and poorly can be very helpful in this regard. Student self-assessments only should be used for formative purposes, not as a basis for determining grades.

HIGH SCHOOL READING PROBLEMS

Developing competent readers is the primary responsibility of elementary school educators. Despite their efforts, however, significant numbers of students enter high school with moderate to serious reading deficits. Allington contends, "We cannot simply stop teaching reading skills and strategies after fourth or fifth grade if we want students to continue to develop as readers" (2006, p. 175). He goes on to note that some students who make progress in reading in the elementary years experience little growth in middle school. When they reach high school they encounter their first real difficulties with reading.

High school reading problems can be especially serious in high poverty urban high schools. Neild and Balfanz (2001) determined that in some of these schools nearly every student needs extra help with reading. The nature of the help, however, varies. Most high school students do not need traditional remedial instruction in basic reading skills that have been covered in the elementary years (Balfanz, McPartland, and Shaw, 2002). Instead, they require help with skills that typically are developed in middle school. Such skills, for example, include the fluency "to simultaneously move smoothly through a complex passage with more advanced vocabulary and apply comprehension strategies to mentally interact with the author's work and accurately derive the intended meaning" (Balfanz, McPartland, and Shaw, 2002, p. 9).

Among the appropriate strategies for School Turnaround Plans that address high school reading problems are the following:

- Creating a continuum of reading interventions
- Training all teachers in how to provide reading assistance
- Adjusting instruction to address the needs of problem readers
- Hiring reading teachers
- Offering reading electives

A continuum of interventions. High schools that are deemed low performing almost always are characterized by a broad range of reading problems.
A few students may lack the most basic components of reading proficiency.
Others have trouble with advanced vocabulary. Still others struggle to make
sense of what they read. Besides variations in reading problems, students also
differ in learning style. Some students respond best to one-on-one assistance.
Others work well in small groups or on a computer. The point is that no
single reading intervention is likely to meet the needs of all struggling readers.

High schools that have implemented a tiered instruction program such
as Response to Intervention already provide a continuum of interventions.
Newly appointed turnaround principals need to work with teachers to make
an inventory of available sources of help for struggling readers. These may
include software programs, special reading series, pullout sessions with specialists, and tutorials. Since the schools in question are low performing, these
existing sources of help clearly are not working for many students. Principals
therefore must determine which sources of help should be adjusted or retained as is and which sources need to be replaced. Principals will require the
expertise of reading specialists to undertake this assessment process.

Training for all teachers. Improvements in reading skills are more likely to
occur when all high school teachers assume responsibility for helping struggling
readers. Biancarosa and Snow (2006) estimate that struggling readers in high
school need approximately two to four hours of literacy instruction each day.
This can only happen when reading assistance is handled as a collective effort.

In order to initiate a "reading across the curriculum" strategy, principals
need to provide teachers with targeted professional development on reading
assistance. If there are reading specialists on the faculty, they may be able to
offer some of this training. Having a specialist model reading assistance in
actual classroom settings is a particularly effective training technique.

Instructional adjustments. The focus of professional development for a high
school faculty should include ways that instruction can be adjusted or supple-
mented to help struggling readers. One useful instructional adjustment involves
preteaching difficult vocabulary prior to introducing a new lesson. Ensuring
that students understand the meaning of key terms *before* they try to comprehend text reduces frustration and the possibility that students will give up.

Another instructional adjustment calls for teachers to provide mini-
lessons periodically during a time when students are reading challenging
written material. Mini-lessons provide brief opportunities to stop reading and

explain difficult concepts, check for understanding, and offer students tools to assist with comprehension (Balfanz, McPartland, and Shaw, 2002). Brevity is crucial to the effectiveness of mini-lessons. The short break from reading helps keep students on task and reduces the chances students become bored.

Matching written materials to student interests and permitting students to select their own reading material are additional methods for adjusting instruction. These techniques increase the likelihood that students enjoy what they are reading and spend more time reading. Reading experts agree that improving reading skills is partly a function of spending more time reading.

Hiring reading teachers. Providing "reading across the curriculum" training for all teachers certainly is important for any effort to improve student reading skills, but it is no substitute for special expertise in reading and literacy. Reading teachers, reading specialists, literacy coaches, and certain special education teachers have the advanced knowledge of reading instruction to provide direct assistance to struggling readers as well as help high school teachers develop skills in teaching reading. These individuals have a major role to play in any effort to develop a continuum of reading interventions.

Reading electives. One option for a continuum of reading interventions is an elective course in reading taught by a specialist. A group of researchers (Showers et al., 1998) found that such a course contributed to impressive gains in reading achievement in one urban high school. Each semester students read five or six books of appropriate difficulty and interest. Instruction in decoding skills for advanced vocabulary was provided along with read-alouds and interactive writing activities. Students who needed it got trained in phonics and structural analysis of text. Offering such help in a credit-bearing elective means that students are able to work on their reading without losing the opportunity to earn a credit toward graduation.

Some high schools provide a Reading and Writing Clinic instead of an elective reading course (Allington, 2006). The benefit of a clinic is that students can drop in on their own or be referred by a teacher on an "as needed" basis, thereby not missing out on taking courses that they require in order to graduate. A clinic should be staffed by a reading specialist whenever possible.

ENGLISH LANGUAGE LEARNERS

It is hardly a surprise that many low-performing schools enroll large numbers of English language learners. These students pose a challenge for teachers who lack an understanding of different cultures and training in how to address the diverse needs of non-English-speakers, some of whom may be illiterate in their native language. The longer it takes for English language learners to acquire proficiency in English, the greater the odds that they will not graduate from high school (English language learners, 2013). It does not help that these students often "are placed in low academic tracks with inexperienced teachers, and many experience pressure to forgo defining elements of their culture and language" (Elfers and Stritikus, 2014, p. 311).

Some of the reading strategies in the previous section as well as the first-order strategy involving general improvement of instruction are certain to serve the interests of English language learners, but there are additional steps that will be required if these students are to succeed. Among the second-order strategies likely to benefit English language learners are the following:

- Structured English immersion
- Shared responsibility for ELLs
- Exposure to core standards and the general curriculum
- Extended learning time
- Parent outreach

Structured English immersion. One strategy gaining traction, though not without controversy, is structured English immersion (SEI). Designed to expedite the learning of English, several states have passed laws requiring SEI and restricting bilingual education (Clark, 2009). While the model for SEI has yet to be fully standardized, it always involves the dedication of significant amounts of the school day to the explicit teaching of the English language. Further, students receiving instruction in English are grouped by their level of proficiency. Grouping in this manner makes it easier for teachers to design focused lessons.

Academic content is covered in SEI, but it is subordinate to English language development (Clark, 2009). Teachers and students are expected to speak, read, and write in English. The notion is that rapid advancement in a language is less likely to occur when learners focus only on oral comprehension. Reading and writing in the language to be acquired speeds up the learning process. Students are expected to complete their SEI instruction based on rigorous timelines. This provision recognizes that English-speaking classmates continue to move forward while English language learners are participating in SEI classes. The shorter the time it takes to acquire basic skill in English, the less academic content English language learners will have to make up. When students exit SEI, they may take a combination of sheltered and mainstream classes until they achieve full proficiency in English.

Shared responsibility for ELLs. When schools implement SEI or other programs where English language learners are segregated for part or all of the school day, mainstream school personnel may assume that addressing the needs of these students is the responsibility of ESL (English as a second language) or ELL (English language learner) teachers. Research indicates, however, that the needs of English language learners are best served when all teachers share responsibility for their education (Rance-Roney, 2009).

Principals can facilitate shared responsibility by establishing cross-disciplinary teams that include content teachers as well as ESL and ELL specialists. Providing these teams with a common planning period increases the likelihood that customized instructional and support plans can be developed and implemented for individual English language learners.

Team members may decide, for example, that certain students are ready to spend a portion of their day in mainstream courses. Team meetings then become occasions when the progress of these students is carefully monitored. Regular monitoring of English language learners' progress has been found to be critical to their long-term success (Williams et al., 2010).

Exposure to core standards and the general curriculum. Seeing that English language learners develop proficiency in English clearly is the highest priority, but it should not become an excuse for exposing these students to a watered-down curriculum. Access as soon as possible to the mainstream curriculum is critical if English language learners are to earn diplomas and possibly attend college.

English language learners sometimes continue to receive assistance in pullout programs long after they have acquired basic English language skills. Principals need to make certain that students are not missing important content tied to core standards when they are pulled out of class. Whenever possible, advancing English language learners should receive support and assistance in their regular class settings. This means that provisions are needed for having specialists work in tandem with content teachers. It also suggests that content teachers should learn techniques for integrating English language learners into their classes.

Another option may be a comprehensive program such as Sheltered Instruction Observation Protocol (SIOP). The SIOP model uses sheltered instruction as a basis for developing English proficiency at the same time that content is made comprehensible (Echevarria, Vogt, and Short, 2014). When appropriate, SIOP allows students' native language to be used. Various teaching methods including modeling, hands-on activities, graphic organizers, and cooperative learning are used to engage students.

Extended learning time. One of the most common strategies for English language learners involves increasing the amount of time that they receive instruction. Extended learning time can be achieved in various ways. A study of California middle schools with track records of success with English language learners identified the following ways of increasing learning time (Williams et al., 2010):

- required extra instructional time during the regular school day, perhaps in place of an elective;
- short-term required interventions that run concurrent with class;
- required intervention time outside the regular school day;
- required intersession or summer courses;
- voluntary academic support offered during nonclassroom time (lunch, after school);
- an online tutorial or intervention program.

It is not enough, however, for principals to create opportunities for extended learning time. They must monitor these opportunities to ensure that students actually are receiving the assistance that they need and that their academic achievement is improving. How these supplementary programs are staffed and with which teachers are critical decisions that go a long way to determining whether supplementary programs are beneficial or a waste of time and resources.

Parent outreach. Principals of schools serving English language learners understand that an effort must be made to welcome and assist parents as well as their school-age children (Elfers and Stritikus, 2014). One effective strategy calls for hiring a parent and community liaison who is fluent in the parents' native language. When parents come from many linguistic backgrounds, it will be necessary to locate interpreters and community members who can function as intermediaries between families and the school. It is especially important for interpreters to be available for the first week of school when incoming students and parents are likely to need assistance navigating their new environment.

Relationship building with the families of English language learners is very important. Home visits by teachers and guidance counselors along with an interpreter help to forge ties between home and school. So, too, do small group gatherings of educators and families in the community. Opening channels of communication is essential so that school-based personnel can learn quickly of issues and concerns that might affect students. To facilitate communication, principals may want to work with district authorities to provide instruction in English for parents of English language learners and to have school newsletters translated into native languages.

Another strategy involves sponsoring school activities that let students and community members know that their native culture is valued. Opportunities to share food, customs, music, and dance serve as valuable learning opportunities for all students and staff as well as an important way to engage parents and community members.

TRANSITION TO NINTH GRADE

Ninth grade is one of the trouble spots in the K–12 school experience for many students. Behavior problems and bad grades are a common occurrence, and retention rates in ninth grade often exceed those at other grade levels (Farrington et al., 2012). Strategies that address the needs of ninth graders can be important components of high school improvement efforts. Ensuring that ninth graders get off on the right foot in high school increases the probability that they will graduate. The following represent some of the strategies that principals of low-performing high schools may want to consider:

- Transition programs
- Ninth grade academies
- Separation of course repeaters
- Close monitoring of progress
- Algebra interventions

Transition programs. Moving from middle school to high school is an anxiety-provoking experience for many teenagers. Just navigating the hallways of a large high school can be daunting. Students frequently struggle to understand what courses they need to take and what teachers expect of them. Teachers in high school sometimes seem less caring than middle school teachers.

Programs designed to orient rising ninth graders to the high school they will attend help to reduce anxiety and make for a smoother transition. While still eighth graders, students can be invited to visit their future high school, meet ninth grade teachers, and even sit in on a few classes. Summer orientation sessions also can be arranged. Nancy Weisskopf developed High School Boot Camp when she was charged with turning around South Hills High School (Duke and Jacobson, 2011). The summer program was run primarily by South Hills juniors and seniors who shared their experiences coming to high school, reviewed school rules, and taught rising ninth graders "the ropes." As a result of the program, each incoming ninth grader came to know several older students to whom they could turn when they needed help.

Another step toward smoother transitions to high school involves close working relations between middle and high school teachers and guidance counselors. Principals should arrange meetings in the spring so that middle school staff members can share information about rising ninth graders and assist with student scheduling and placement.

Ninth grade academies. Transition programs help rising ninth graders build awareness of the rigors of high school. Ninth grade or freshman academies ensure that students get the support needed to handle high school academics (Thompson et al., 2011). Also referred to as houses, ninth grade academies function apart from the rest of the high school. Groups of students typically are taught core courses by the same team of teachers, much like they may have been taught in middle school. The academy usually is assigned a guidance counselor and possibly a special education teacher.

Separating ninth graders from upperclassmen makes it easier to adjust student schedules and arrange special programs to address areas of academic weakness, particularly in English and mathematics. Separation also reduces the social pressure that can result from interactions with older students. Ninth grade academies ideally are located in a separate building on campus or a separate wing or floor of the high school.

Principals who opt for a ninth grade academy should exercise great care in staffing it. Experienced teachers with an understanding of both the middle school and ninth grade curriculum are preferable to novice teachers.

Separation of course repeaters. When ninth grade academies are in operation, only incoming ninth graders take classes together as a rule. In the absence of a separate ninth grade program, freshmen often wind up taking classes with course repeaters. Students who fail a course and have to retake it do not make good role models for first timers. They also can be disruptive and inattentive. Handling repeaters often results in the loss of valuable instructional time.

Nancy Weisskopf established a policy at South Hills High School that prevented repeaters from taking classes with first timers. Repeaters were required to retake courses online in a computer lab where they worked independently. In 2013, Washington's District of Columbia Public Schools established a district-wide policy of separating first timers and repeaters in freshman classes.

Close monitoring of progress. The level of academic work expected in high school can come as a shock to many freshmen. Homework often is more demanding, and tests require greater thought and precision. School Turnaround Plans targeting ninth graders need provisions for closely monitoring student work. At the first sign of problems, teachers should provide assistance—not allow days and weeks to pass before intervening.

One strategy that Nancy Weisskopf insisted on was a "no failure" policy for ninth graders. Rather than allowing ninth graders to choose to fail by no longer trying hard in class and falling behind in assignments, students were required to take time during school hours to get caught up. "Just Do It" days, as indicated earlier, were monitored by South Hills assistant principals. If more time was needed, ninth graders were required to stay after school for an hour a day until they received the assistance they needed to catch up with their classmates. If the students were still behind when school ended in the late spring, they continued to come to school until they completed the work needed to pass their classes.

Close monitoring of student progress becomes much easier when teachers working with ninth graders regularly meet to discuss students who are struggling and devise ways to provide help. When all the teachers who work with a particular student can offer support and assistance, the student gets the message that they are cared about.

Algebra interventions. Probably no course causes ninth graders more concern than Algebra 1. It is required for graduation in all states and is considered essential for collegebound students. While some states and school districts encourage students to complete Algebra 1 in the eighth grade or earlier, the norm is still for ninth graders to take the course. Struggling with Algebra 1 can cause ninth graders to abandon the goal of going to college and lose interest in academic work in general.

With regard to taking Algebra before high school, several studies indicate that students who have difficulty with math derive no benefit in terms of scores on state math tests (Sparks, 2012). What's more, early Algebra for struggling students hurts their grade point averages and reduces the likelihood of their taking and passing higher level math courses in high school.

When students who struggle with math in middle school become high school freshmen, they are likely to need assistance with Algebra. One strategy that has yielded encouraging results is to give low-achievers a double dose of Algebra 1 (Durwood, Krone, and Mazzeo, 2010). Chicago implemented double dosing in addition to support for Algebra teachers in the form of professional development. Regular Algebra class was followed immediately by Algebra support class. Both classes were taught by the same teacher and involved the same students. Test scores rose significantly for double dosers. It is important to note that Algebra teachers also changed the way they taught Algebra, making greater use of interactive teaching methods and differentiated instruction. At least in the case of Algebra, the controversial policy of homogeneous grouping by ability made a positive difference.

Principals of low-performing schools who are unable to implement double dosing in Algebra at least should provide opportunities for Algebra teachers to upgrade their skills in teaching low-achievers. Effective instruction for low-achievers involves the use of meaningful problems that engage student interest, explicit instruction in foundational knowledge and skills, use of students' prior knowledge and intuitions, and shared dialogue regarding challenging math tasks (Balfanz, McPartland, and Shaw, 2002). Interventions that make use of correct and incorrect examples (Booth et al., 2013) and engaging computer applications (Okur et al., 2011) also have yielded promising results.

DROPOUTS

Most of the second-order strategies presented in the preceding pages are capable of reducing the likelihood that students will drop out of high school. Any strategy that helps students succeed in elementary, middle, and high school is an investment in dropout prevention. High school principals may want to consider additional strategies if significant numbers of students fail to graduate. They include the following:

- Personalized learning environments
- Credit tracking
- Adult advocates
- Credit recovery programs
- Career and technical education

Personalized learning environments. When researchers interviewed high school dropouts, they found that large numbers of them reported having no teacher or staff member who personally cared about their success or to whom they could go to talk about school and personal problems (Bridgeland, Dilulio, and Morison, 2006). Responses of this kind led the Institute of Education Sciences (Dynarski et al., 2008) to recommend the development of personalized learning environments as a way to reduce the likelihood that students drop out of high school.

Large high schools can be impersonal environments where some students simply fall through the cracks. Keeping teacher-student ratios low certainly is one way to cultivate a more inviting atmosphere. Ninth grade academies accomplish this goal by clustering the same group of students with a team of teachers for a significant portion of the school day. Such clustering can extend beyond the ninth grade as well. In some urban districts such as New York and Chicago, large high schools have been purposely subdivided into smaller high schools, each with its own faculty and often with a unique academic or vocational focus.

Neild, Stoner-Eby, and Furstenberg (2008) found that students who spend time in special education programs are less likely to drop out of high school. They speculated that the reason may have to do with the smaller, often self-contained classes that special education students experience. Such settings allow for closer relationships with teachers and greater student attachment to school.

Credit tracking. Students who struggle in high school often fail to keep track of the number of credits they have earned or the remaining credits they need to graduate. This can lead to unpleasant "surprises" in junior and senior year. Students who discover that they have little chance of earning enough credits to graduate are more likely to drop out of high school.

When Anabel Garza took over as turnaround principal of Reagan High School in Austin, Texas, she discovered that guidance counselors were not tracking students' accumulation of credits needed for graduation (Duke and Jacobson, 2011). To make matters worse, students sometimes were placed in classes that either they had taken before or that they did not need for graduation. Guidance staff seemed to be interested primarily in finding a place to stick students who were struggling academically. The situation at Reagan is not atypical of low-performing high schools. One of Garza's first actions was to instruct guidance counselors to closely track credit accumulation for every student, to keep students and parents informed of progress, and to stop assigning students to classes that did not lead to graduation credits.

One proven comprehensive prevention strategy that places emphasis on close monitoring of credit accumulation along with academic performance is Check & Connect (*Check & Connect*, 2006). This strategy also calls for case management of struggling students, mentoring, family and community agency engagement, and other student supports. Mentors regularly discuss the importance of learning and staying in school with mentees. Students also are taught a five-step plan for handling problems that they encounter in and outside of school.

Adult advocates. As already noted, many high school students feel that there is no adult to whom they can turn when they have school and personal problems. A strategy that has been found to be effective in reducing student isolation involves assigning a person to work individually with individuals at risk of dropping out (Dynarski et al., 2008). More than a mentor, this person serves as a case manager, offering guidance on both school and out-of-school matters, modeling positive behavior and sound decision-making skills, and taking an active interest in the student's success. An advocate can be a resource teacher, community member, or social worker. Principals must make certain that advocates have the proper qualities to be good role models and the training needed to be effective. Advocates may need help in identifying the local resources available to at-risk teenagers and their families.

Credit recovery programs. For students who are not overage but seriously deficient in the credits needed to graduate and motivated to catch up, the only hope is a well-structured credit recovery program. These programs usually are run outside of the regular school day, since students still have to continue attending school and earning credits. Some credit recovery programs are run during late afternoons and evenings, but the best time for them is in the summer. Completing courses online also is a possibility now that many states have developed such options.

Fred C. Beyer High School in Modesto, California, adopted a variation on this strategy. An alternative program was set up for former dropouts and students who were behind in the credits needed to graduate. Students learn in small groups and on their own in settings designed like office workspaces. Students have the option to attend four-hour "shifts" in the morning, afternoon, and evening. The more shifts they attend, the faster they can complete the requirements to graduate.

It is essential for credit recovery programs to be staffed with teachers who are capable of helping students overcome academic and personal problems. Some students may require help with reading comprehension, while others may be poor time managers. Whatever their issues, a competent and caring staff is needed to support students through the process of making up deficient credits. Credit recovery should not be an excuse, however, for providing students with a dumbed-down curriculum and shallow learning experience.

Career and technical education. When researchers asked dropouts what would have improved their chances of staying in school and eventually graduating, a whopping 81 percent cited more opportunities for relevant, real-world learning experiences (Bridgeland, Dilulio, and Morison, 2006). Career and technical education (CTE) can be the ideal strategy for providing such experiences. Career Pathways is a CTE strategy that provides students with a series of connected education and training experiences to enable them to earn industry certification and obtain employment within an occupational area. Federal funding is available to support many school-based CTE initiatives.

An on-the-job internship, one that may enable students to earn a salary, coupled with courses during part of each day can be attractive to some students. Having a chance to function in the adult world while also completing courses for a diploma is especially important for young people who must help to support their families.

This chapter only scratches the surface when it comes to second-order strategies. The discussion of dropout prevention strategies, for example, included nothing about Performance Learning Centers, AVID (Advancement Via Individual Determination), Early College High Schools, and overage academies for students between eighteen and twenty-one years of age. The aim of the chapter was simply to point out that principals and others involved in developing School Turnaround Plans should never jump at the first strategy that seems to fit a goal or objective. A variety of possibilities should be identified and considered before committing to a particular strategy. Principals must be prepared to explain why one strategy was preferred over others.

REFERENCES

Allington, R. L. 2006. *What Really Matters for Struggling Readers,* 2nd ed. Boston: Pearson.

Balfanz, R.; McPartland, J.; and Shaw, A. 2002. *Reconceptualizing Extra Help for High School Students in a High Standards Era.* Baltimore, MD: The Johns Hopkins University, Center for Social Organization of Schools.

Bandura, A. 1997. *Self-Efficacy: The Exercise of Control.* New York: Freeman.

Biancarosa, C. and Snow, C. E. 2006. *Reading Next: A Vision for Action and Research in Middle and High School Literacy: A Report to Carnegie Corporation of New York.* Washington, DC: Alliance for Excellent Education.

Booth, J.; Lange, K.; Koedinger, K.; and Newton, K. 2013. Using example problems to improve student learning in algebra: Differentiating between correct and incorrect examples. *Learning and Instruction,* 25(1), 24–34.

Bridgeland, J. M.; Dilulio, J. J.; and Morison, K. B. 2006. *The Silent Epidemic: Perspectives of High School Dropouts.* Washington, DC: Civic Enterprises.

Check & Connect. 2006. Washington, DC: What Works Clearinghouse, Institute of Education Sciences, U.S. Department of Education.

Clark, K. 2009. The case for structured English immersion. *Educational Leadership,* 66(7), 42–46.

Diplomas count. June 6, 2013. *Education Week.*

Duke, D. L. and Jacobson, M. 2011. Tackling the toughest turnaround—low-performing high schools. *Kappan,* 92(5), 34–38.

Durwood, C.; Krone, E.; and Mazzeo, C. 2010. *Are Two Algebra Classes Better Than One? The Effects of Double-Dose Instruction in Chicago.* Chicago: Consortium for Chicago School Research, University of Chicago.

Dweck, C. S.; Walton, G. M.; and Cohen, G. L. 2011. *Academic Tenacity: Mindsets and Skills that Promote Long-Term Learning.* White paper prepared for the Gates Foundation. Seattle, WA: Gates Foundation.

Dynarski, M.; Clarke, L.; Cobb, B.; Finn, J.; Rumberger, R.; and Smink, J. 2008. *Dropout Prevention: A Practice Guide.* Washington, DC: Institute of Education Sciences, U.S. Department of Education.

Echevarria, J. J.; Vogt, M.; and Short, D. J. 2014. *Making Content Comprehensible for English Learners: The SIOP Model,* 4th ed. Boston: Pearson.

Elfers, A. M. and Stritikus, T. 2014. How school and district leaders support classroom teachers' work with English language learners. *Educational Administration Quarterly,* 50(2), 305–344.

English language learners. 2013. *The Progress of Education Reform,* 14(6). Education Commission of the States.

Farrington, C. A.; Roderick, M.; Allensworth, E.; Nagaoka, J.; Keyes, T. S.; Johnson, D. W.; and Beechum, N. O. 2012. *Teaching Adolescents to Become Learners.* Chicago: Consortium for Chicago School Research, University of Chicago.

Hulleman, C. S. and Harackiewicz, J. M. 2009. Making education relevant: Increasing interest and performance in high school science classes. *Science,* 326, 1410–1412.

Improving School Attendance. 2005. Richmond, VA: Virginia Department of Education.

Le, C. and Wolfe, R. E. 2013. How can schools boost students' self-regulation? *Kappan,* 95(2), 33–38.

Neild, R. C. and Balfanz, R. 2001. *An Extreme Degree of Difficulty: The Educational Demographics of the Ninth Grade in Philadelphia.* Baltimore, MD: The Johns Hopkins University, Center for Social Organization of Schools.

Neild, R. C; Stoner-Eby, S.; and Furstenberg, F. 2008. Connecting entrance and departure: The transition to ninth grade and high school dropout. *Education and Urban Society,* 40(5), 543–569.

Okur, M.; Dikici, R.; Sanalan, V.; and Tatar, E. 2011. Computer applications in teaching abstract algebra. *International Journal of Applied Science and Technology,* 1(1), 20–27.

Rance-Roney, J. 2009. Best Practices for adolescent ELLs. *Educational Leadership,* 66(7), 32– 37.

Showers, B.; Joyce, B.; Scanlon, M.; and Schnaubelt, C. 1998. A second chance to learn to read. *Educational Leadership,* 72(1), 27–30.

Sparks, S. D. April 25, 2012. Researchers suggest early algebra harmful to struggling students. *Education Week,* 10.

Steele, C. M. 2010. *Whistling Vivaldi.* New York: W. W. Norton.

Stiggins, R. J. 2005. *Student-Involved Assessment FOR Learning,* 4th ed. Upper Saddle River, NJ: Pearson.

Thompson, C. L.; Brown, K. M.; Townsend, L. W.; Henry, G. T.; and Fortner, C. K. 2011. *Turning Around North Carolina's Lowest Achieving Schools* (2006–2010). Chapel Hill, NC: Consortium for Educational Research and Evaluation—North Carolina.

Tough, P. 2012. *How Children Succeed.* Boston: Houghton Mifflin Harcourt.

Williams, T.; Kirst, M.; Haertel, E.; et al. 2010. *Gaining Ground In The Middle Grades: Why Some Schools Do Better.* Mountain View, CA: EdSource.

Willingham, D. T. 2009. *Why Don't Students Like School?* San Francisco: Jossey-Bass.

7

Setting the Stage for a New Beginning

This chapter examines the period between the time that an individual is presented with the opportunity to turn around a low-performing school and the beginning of the new school year. The "individual" could be the current principal, but he or she is just as likely to be a new leader. Little has been written about this time before school starts, but it is a critical time in the turnaround process. Writing about such periods in the business world, Watkins (2003) points out that small differences in a new leader's early actions can have a disproportionate impact on outcomes. He goes on to note, "Leaders . . . are most vulnerable in their first few months in a new position because they lack detailed knowledge of the challenges they will face and what it will take to succeed in meeting them" (p. ix).

Some of the most important challenges of these early months, typically during the summer when school is not in session, will be discussed in this chapter. It will help if you try to imagine filling the shoes of a newly appointed principal of a low-performing school as they gear up for the opening of school and the launching of a school turnaround initiative. Toward this end, the second person pronoun will be used throughout the chapter.

The first challenge you will confront involves determining whether or not to accept the job of turnaround principal. Before agreeing, you will need to meet with the superintendent or their designee and negotiate the conditions of your job. Assuming you accept the job, subsequent challenges will include developing your leadership team, reviewing the school's most recent improvement plan, filling vacant positions, meeting stakeholders, undertaking some "quick wins," and planning the kick-off to the new school year. Each of these challenges will be examined in the chapter.

PRELIMINARY CHALLENGES

1. Negotiating the conditions of the job
2. Developing the leadership team
3. Reviewing the most recent improvement plan
4. Filling vacant positions
5. Meeting stakeholders
6. Undertaking "quick wins"
7. Planning the kick-off to the new school year

JOB NEGOTIATIONS

You receive a phone call indicating that you have been selected to serve as principal of a school designated for turnaround. Now what?

The time between the phone call and when you sign a contract can be of immense importance. You have been chosen over other candidates. The school system wants you. You will never be in a better position to negotiate for additional resources to assist in the turnaround process. You already understand that some "quick wins" are crucial for building momentum for change and for demonstrating to skeptics that you know how to get things done. At this early date, you may not know exactly what quick wins to pursue, but whatever they turn out to be, they will require extra resources.

Before you discuss resources, however, you need to get as clear an idea as possible of what is expected of you. Are you expected, for example, to replace large numbers of teachers? If so, what support can you expect from the central office? Has the superintendent set achievement targets for your school? If so, what are they, and how long do you have to reach them? How much discretionary authority will you be allotted when it comes to developing the School Turnaround Plan? Who must approve the plan? How closely will the central office monitor progress?

One of the surest ways to determine how much support to expect from the central office is to review your school's budget with the appropriate district authorities. Is there room for adjustment? What if you decide to add a literacy coach or a math specialist to the faculty? Can that be arranged? How about capital improvements, say a new coat of paint for the school or some attractive plantings to enhance the school's appearance?

If district authorities are unwilling to commit to such requests, you may want to reconsider taking the job. Successful turnarounds depend on additional resources early on in the process. A retreat for the faculty before school opens. New textbooks. Laptops for a credit recovery program. More teachers to lower the teacher-student ratio. Removal of graffiti. District authorities, of course, cannot give you a blank check, but they should understand that you will need some additional funding, or at least the latitude to adjust the existing budget.

When Roberto Loredo became principal of Memorial High School in Alamo, Texas, he knew what was needed right off the bat (Clubine et al., 2001). Students coming to Memorial represented various levels of achievement. A modified block schedule would provide opportunities for students who needed extra time to get the assistance they required. Loredo obtained the support of the central office and implemented the new schedule, the only block schedule at the time in the Pharr-San Juan-Alamo Independent School District. Classes meet for ninety minutes each day. This means that many courses can be completed in eighteen weeks, an advantage for students who may need to repeat a course. Certain courses, such as Algebra, Geometry, and English II, require thirty-six weeks, however.

Central office support is critical to the success of any school turnaround initiative. No candidate for the position of turnaround principal should accept the job without knowing the kind of support they can count on. Chapter 10 looks in greater depth at what district leaders can do to bolster the efforts of turnaround principals.

SCHOOL LEADERSHIP TEAM

A newly elected President of the United States gets to create his own Cabinet, but many turnaround principals inherit their predecessor's leadership team. One or more team members even may have competed for the position that you won. You do not necessarily have to stick with team members over the long haul. Until you know who you can and cannot count on, though, it may be necessary to work with the existing team.

Assuming that you agree to sign the contract and become principal of a low-performing school, one of the first things you will need to do is meet individually with each member of the leadership team. Chances are that you will have met the team members when you interviewed for the job. You now need to find out what their actual responsibilities are and how these compare to their written job descriptions. It is also important to determine how each team member feels about the work they do.

You should convene the leadership team well before the beginning of the new school year. Individuals who are not on annual contracts may need to be paid a stipend for their time. Funding for stipends is another example of the kind of resources you should request before agreeing to be principal. An excellent activity for the first meeting of the leadership team is a review of the previous year's School Improvement Plan. You will want to gather opinions about what goals and objectives were and were not achieved and the reasons why. This activity naturally leads into thinking about the School Turnaround Plan for the upcoming school year.

Before launching into developing the new School Turnaround Plan, however, you should review the components of a sound plan. Hopefully this book has provided you with lots of tips in this regard. You also may want to secure the services of an outside expert to assist with developing the team's planning and data-analysis skills.

Because the development of a School Turnaround Plan consists of various steps and the time for planning in the summer is brief, you need to create an Action Plan with a specific date for completing each step. Figure 7.1 provides an example of an Action Plan for developing the initial 90-day plan for a school turnaround initiative. The plan includes the activities that must be completed, the purpose of each activity, and the date by which the activity must be accomplished.

Turnaround Tip: Because the summer can be a busy time for principals, create a step-by-step Action Plan to guide the development of the School Turnaround Plan.

Table 7.1. Sample Summer Action Plan

Goal: Develop a 90-Day School Turnaround Plan to Launch the School Turnaround Process

Completion Date	Activity	Purpose
July 3	Review previous school year's School Improvement Plan with leadership team.	Identify unachieved goals and strategies that did not work.
July 10	Analyze results of spring state testing with leadership team.	Identify areas of academic weakness.
July 24	Meet with stakeholder focus groups (faculty members, central office experts, students, etc.).	Determine possible reasons for academic problems and lack of success with previous School Improvement Plan.
July 27	Analyze feedback from stakeholder groups and develop a tentative set of goals for the coming school year.	Begin the process of developing the first 90-day plan.
August 1	Collect additional data and reactions to tentative goals for first 90-day plan.	Determine if causes of academic problems are understood and if general agreement exists regarding goals for first 90-day plan.
August 15	Complete first 90-day plan by refining goals, identifying objectives for each goal, choosing strategies for each objective, specifying resources required to implement strategies, and creating a timeline for each strategy's implementation.	Focus human and material resources for the initial phase of the turnaround process.
August 22	Share 90-day plan with superintendent's cabinet.	Obtain constructive feedback, secure permission to proceed with plan, and request any additional resources needed to implement plan.
August 29	Present 90-day plan to faculty and parent groups.	Officially launch the turnaround process.

The sample Action Plan begins with a review by the leadership team of the previous year's School Improvement Plan. It is important to know what the goals were for this plan, the strategies that were supposed to be implemented to achieve the goals, how well these strategies were implemented, and what was actually achieved. Listening to team members discuss these matters should provide a new principal with insight into how team members think about their school and efforts to raise student achievement.

Assuming the results of state testing in the spring are available, the next step for the leadership team involves analyzing test results to determine where students are improving, holding steady, and declining. This information will help in the identification of improvement targets for the coming year's School Turnaround Plan.

The results of spring testing should be shared with groups of stakeholders in order to get their insights into why students struggled with some test content more than other content. It is not possible to gather every teacher, central office specialist, and student in the summer, but focus groups probably can be arranged on relatively short notice. Their responses should be recorded for subsequent use in developing the first 90-day plan.

The next step for leadership team members calls for reflection on stakeholder input and the identification of a focused set of tentative student achievement goals for the coming school year. Once these goals have been specified, team members may need to collect additional information before they start searching for strategies. They could decide, for instance, that data on attendance would be helpful. Or they might want to break down student achievement by individual teachers. The purpose of collecting additional data at this point is to narrow the range of possible causes of low achievement.

Getting teachers' reactions to the draft set of goals also will be important at this point. Faculty members are more likely to embrace goals that they have had a chance to consider before plans are finalized.

Completing the initial 90-day plan is the next step. This means focusing on a small number of priority goals, specifying objectives for each goal, identifying strategies related to each objective, determining the resources required to implement each strategy, and creating timelines for implementation. Because it is mid-August at this point and the time for completing initial planning is short, team members should be assigned to work on different goals rather than trying to conduct all plan development with the team as a whole.

The most challenging part of plan development probably will be agreeing on strategies. Team members in low-performing schools often feel that everything possible has been tried without achieving desired results. Just because lots of strategies have been attempted, however, does not mean they have been executed well or used in a coherent and strategic way (Finnigan and Stewart, 2009). Principals, for example, sometimes move immediately to second-order strategies, forgetting that first-order strategies provide the foundations for the effective implementation of second-order strategies. It is imperative for you to understand as much as possible about why particular strategies did not work before completing the new School Turnaround Plan.

The leadership team may decide to come up with two plans, a full year-long School Turnaround Plan and a 90-day plan to cover the first phase of the yearlong plan. Team members must understand, however, that the key to success lies in continuous planning, not just producing a plan or two. The last steps in the Action Plan involve sharing the final plan or plans with district authorities, gaining their approval, and presenting the plan to the faculty and other stakeholders.

Besides developing a plan for turning around the school, the leadership team should devote time over the summer to reviewing the existing School Discipline Plan and the Crisis Management Plan. Safety and order are the highest priorities and must not be taken for granted. When I asks my students to review their schools' plans, they often discover that portions of the plans are out-of-date.

Since you are new to the school, you need to become familiar with the procedures for handling critical incidents, the individuals assigned responsibilities for helping to handle emergencies, and the kinds of safety problems that have occurred at the school. At least one team member should be assigned responsibility for updating the School Discipline Plan and the Crisis Management Plan.

SUMMER HIRING

The teacher turnover rate in low-performing schools can be very high. Even if the conditions of your school turnaround do not require the replacement of a large percentage of the faculty, you can expect to fill various positions over the summer. As a newly appointed principal, you will not have much time to recruit teachers. The chances are that you will have to work with candidates who already have applied for positions in the district and not been hired elsewhere or teachers who recently decided to transfer.

What will you look for when selecting new faculty members? Obviously you want individuals with a sound knowledge of the subject matter they will be required to teach. But turning around a low-performing school will require more than content knowledge. Teachers must understand how to reach students who may not be highly motivated and who may be behind grade level in reading ability. This means that candidates must be patient and well-organized. They must be able to provide clear directions, convey high expectations, and know how to manage student behavior so that valuable instructional time is not lost handling discipline. It also helps for teachers to possess some understanding of the cultural backgrounds of their students and the conditions in which they live.

Content knowledge, instructional skill, and cultural awareness are not the only critical requirements. Because turning around a low-performing school requires collective effort, candidates must be able to collaborate and function effectively in teams. Finding out how candidates feel about team-based planning, data analysis, and student assistance should be a part of the interview process.

Nancy Weisskopf had to hire dozens of new teachers when she launched the turnaround process at South Hills High School. She was very clear about what she was looking for in applicants. Each applicant was asked, "Failure is not an option. What does it mean to you?" (Duke, 2011). Weisskopf knew what she wanted to hear in response. She wanted teachers who were committed to never giving up on a student. She found the teachers she was looking for, but it required more than 360 interviews!

Requirements such as those in the preceding paragraphs constitute a tall order for any school, much less a low-performing school. With veteran teachers, you might be able to speak with their previous principals to get an idea of their competence and commitment, but low-performing schools often get more applicants who are recent graduates than experienced teachers. As in so many aspects of leading a low-performing school, your judgment may have to substitute for high-quality data. The chances of making the right judgment will be enhanced, however, by having candidates meet with faculty members, especially those with whom candidates might be working. Asking candidates to design a sample lesson and teach a lesson to a summer school class also can provide useful information.

If you have reservations about some applicants and time is running out, the most prudent decision may be to offer them long-term substitute contracts. This allows you to continue searching for highly qualified teachers while you give the individuals a chance to prove themselves.

Newly hired teachers will need an induction program to familiarize them with the school's needs and your expectations. Induction gatherings typically begin before school starts and continue throughout the school year. Besides socialization and professional development, the induction process offers an opportunity for new teachers to discuss concerns and ask questions. Another important purpose of induction sessions is community building. If you want to retain good teachers, you must help them to feel that they are members of a supportive professional family.

Newly hired teachers should be provided with an induction program to promote collaboration and offer ongoing support.

Mentors also can be a valuable source of support for new teachers, but care should be exercised in matching new teachers and veteran teacher mentors. Pairing pessimistic and burned-out teachers with young and energetic novices can be an unpleasant and frustrating experience. If no one on the faculty fills the bill for a mentor, it may be best to find a district instructional coach willing to help.

When it comes to the veteran faculty members who already are on the faculty, you need to review their previous evaluations and observations in order to become familiar with any issues that may have arisen in the past. Of particular importance is whether certain teachers have been or currently are on formal plans of assistance. A candid conversation with your predecessor can provide additional insights that may not appear in personnel files.

RELATIONSHIP BUILDING

One of the most important keys to the successful implementation of first-order and second-order strategies is the relationships that you are able to build with members of your staff, students, parents, and central office personnel. Positive and trusting relations facilitate the change process. Negative relations characterized by distrust and animosity subvert the change process. Covey (1994) warns that relationship building is one of those activities that leaders often deem to be important but non-urgent. He advises leaders not to allow the urgent always to push relationship building to the back burner. Doing so can sow the seeds for future problems.

Longitudinal research on efforts to improve Chicago elementary schools found that principals of schools where student achievement gains were made attended to two basic ideas (Bryk et al., 2010). The first involved a strategic focus on improving teaching and learning. The second key idea entailed grounding improvement strategies in efforts to build trusting relationships across the school community. Relational trust between principals and teachers, teachers and parents, and teachers and other teachers was found to be greater in the high-gain schools.

What does it mean for trusting relationships to exist between principals and teachers? In the Chicago study, it meant transparency regarding issues and concerns, mutual respect, and personal regard. Teachers also felt that the principal valued their expertise.

Trust, of course, is not built overnight. Still, you need to begin building trust and positive relationships with stakeholders as soon as possible. Turnaround principals often try to meet individually with as many teachers as possible before school begins. Some also conduct home visits in order to get to know parents. Having an interpreter on hand when visiting non-English-speaking parents obviously is important.

Not to be neglected are relationships with key central office personnel. This is especially important in large, highly bureaucratized school districts. Make a point of getting to know top administrators in the human relations, transportation, purchasing, technology, and facilities management departments. Be sure to identify the individual in each unit that you have to contact when a problem arises or you need a quick response to a question.

—❈—

Turnaround Tip: Make a point of identifying key contacts in central office units that provide services to your school.

—❈—

The school's office staff plays a critical role in relationship building. Because turnover of professional staff in low-performing schools often is high, office staff may have longer years of experience at the school than most teachers and administrators. Frequently they live near the school and know many of the students' families.

If office staff are not welcoming to parents, students, and other visitors, it is a direct reflection on your leadership (or lack of leadership). When Anabel Garza arrived for her first day as principal of Reagan High School, she was appalled that no one in the front office bothered to greet her or ask who she was (Duke and Jacobson, 2011). She began to understand why there had been complaints by parents and students that they were not well treated when they sought help from office staff. One of Garza's first acts as principal involved hiring a friend from a hotel chain to conduct an inservice on hospitality and client service for the office staff.

When you work with your office staff, you need to provide clear directions about how they are to deal with the public, handle phone inquiries and complaints, and treat student requests. Designate someone to keep a written record of problems reported to the office, questions asked by current and prospective parents, and other matters that require your attention. When you are not available to respond to requests and problems, let office staff know to whom to refer such matters. It is essential that these relatively routine operational issues be worked out before the beginning of school.

PLANNING QUICK WINS

The early days of leading a low-performing school to improvement is largely about building momentum. Failure to generate momentum can undo even the most carefully planned turnaround initiative. Momentum is needed to counteract the cynicism and demoralization that can develop over the years in low-performing schools. Veteran teachers and community members begin to believe that nothing can be done to raise achievement. Faith in leadership flags.

To restore faith in leadership and start boosting confidence that positive change is possible, you will need to accomplish some quick wins. These small victories often begin before students return to school. Efforts to make the school and its surroundings more attractive was mentioned earlier. So, too, was hiring additional staff.

When Nancy Blackwell took over as principal of Hambrick Middle School, a struggling school in Aldine, Texas, she immediately undertook several actions designed to show people that she could get things done to improve life at Hambrick (Picucci et al., 2002). First she got the maintenance department to clean up the school, fix broken light fixtures, and replace chairs in the auditorium. It is hard for students and teachers to take pride in a school that looks like a dump.

Later, when classes resumed, Blackwell made certain that displays of student work covered school walls. Seeing a clean and attractive school prompted students to pitch in and help keep their environment from returning to its previous sorry state.

Blackwell also focused on making certain that teachers had the resources they needed to begin the new school year. In previous years, teachers sometimes waited for supplies until late fall and beyond. Getting colored pencils for math students may not seem like a quick win to those working in affluent school systems, but to Hambrick's math teachers it was a sign that the new principal cared. Little victories pave the way to larger victories.

Hambrick had a reputation for disorder, especially during passing times between classes. Students often lingered at their lockers and were late getting to classes. Blackwell decided to establish a new procedure for changing classes. The sounding of bells was eliminated. Students were grouped by academic team and assigned to classes located on the same corridor. When the time came to change classes, teachers escorted students into the hallway and supervised their movement to the next class. Blackwell also eliminated the use of hall lockers under the pretense of needing to paint the lockers. No longer having the excuse of stopping at their lockers between classes, students got to classes on time, another quick win. Disruptive incidents in the halls were reduced as well.

Another example of a quick win comes from the early days of Nancy Warren's principalship at Baskin Elementary School in San Antonio, Texas (Johnson and Acera, 1999). Warren knew that there had been little collaboration among Baskin teachers before she arrived. To promote a team approach to turning around the school, she converted a large classroom in the center of the school into a teacher workroom. More than a typical cramped work space with a copier and a work table, the spacious new workroom resembled a conference room. A number of tables were available for individual projects, but they easily could be converted into a large set of connecting tables for group meetings. The room contained a professional library as well. Teachers regarded the creation of the new workroom as a vote of confidence in their ability to work together for the improvement of Baskin.

Creating a teacher workroom and making certain teachers have the supplies they need *before* school begins are quick wins sure to score points with faculty members. What about parents and students? Because of student mobility and lack of parent understanding of the registration process, the first weeks of school can find significant numbers of students unassigned to classes (Duke and Jacobson, 2011; Picucci et al., 2002). Working with students, parents, and guidance counselors to make certain that every student has classes to attend on the first day of school as well as a roadmap to graduation can go a long way to ensuring that the school year gets off to a good start.

Nancy Weisskopf won over students by soliciting their input when she launched South Hills's turnaround (Duke and Jacobson, 2011). Weisskopf felt it was important to rebrand the school as a way of signaling a new beginning. Students got to choose a new mascot—a scorpion—and new school colors. "Scorpion Pride" posters soon adorned the hallways, and Weisskopf became the "Scorpion Queen."

What you would do to achieve quick wins obviously depends on many things, including your school's culture, the resources available to you as a new principal, and what stakeholders regard as important. Just one cautionary note: Avoid undertaking more quick wins than can be accomplished in a short period of time. No one in a low-performing school needs the disappointment that comes with failed attempts to improve their school.

———

Turnaround Tip: Achieving some quick wins to build confidence and momentum is important at the outset, but be careful not to attempt more quick wins than actually can be accomplished.

———

KICKING OFF THE NEW SCHOOL YEAR

After all the preparations of the summer—building the leadership team, developing the School Turnaround Plan, hiring, and so on—you probably will be anxious to get the turnaround process into high gear. Investing some thought in how to conduct your back-to-school meeting with the entire faculty will pay dividends later. Think about what needs to be accomplished at this initial gathering of the individuals who will be directly responsible for raising student achievement. New teachers and veterans need to get to know each other. Some faculty members may not have met you yet, so they will want to know something about your beliefs and intentions. The School Turnaround Plan will need to be introduced along with a discussion of its implications for individual teachers, grade-level groups, and academic departments. Any new policies and procedures must be explained. Teachers will require time to organize their classrooms and prepare for the arrival of students.

Try to imagine what will be on the minds of teachers. They will want to know what is going to be different about the coming school year. How will the new plan for improving student outcomes be different from past plans?

Depending on the size of the faculty, it may be best to limit the length of the school-wide meeting and divide into grade-level or subject-matter groups in order to handle matters of specific concern to particular groups. If project management teams have been formed to address objectives in the School Turnaround Plan, they will need time to meet as well. More will be said about these teams in the next chapter.

Turning around a low-performing school is serious business, but that doesn't mean people cannot have some fun along the way. Time should be set aside during back-to-school days for the entire school staff to engage in some not-so-serious activities. A pot-luck dinner where everyone prepares food together, a treasure hunt, and a softball game can be occasions for laughter, bonding, and team building.

You also should consider how to welcome back students and parents. They, too, will want to know about the plans to boost achievement. Students and parents should feel like they are an integral part of school improvement efforts. Engaging students right off the bat in some activity related to the turnaround initiative can be an important signal that things are changing. Choosing a new mascot or developing a new school slogan are two activities sometimes undertaken by students in turnaround schools. Letting students and parents know about specific roles that they can play in school improvement efforts also is a good idea.

You may want to publicize academic achievement targets for particular grade levels as well as the entire school and enlist students in the campaign to reach or exceed the targets. Handled in the right way, students respond well to such challenges. They actually may be more willing to work hard for the sake of their school's reputation than for their own success. Turnaround principals often find that appealing to student's loyalty to their school is a powerful motivator.

———∞∞∞———

Turnaround Tip: Students and parents appreciate knowing what role they can play in helping to turn around their school.

———∞∞∞———

By the time teachers and students return to school, you may feel like you already have put in a full year's work. Your summer's efforts focused on making certain that the new school year gets off to an auspicious beginning and that the school community gains a clear sense of the direction in which the school is headed. The next steps in the turnaround process involve implementing the School Turnaround Plan and ensuring that achievement gains are made. These steps are addressed in the next chapter.

REFERENCES

Bryk, A. S.; Sebring, P. B.; Allensworth, E.; Luppescu, S.; and Easton, J. Q. 2010. *Organizing Schools for Improvement.* Chicago: University of Chicago Press.

Clubine, B.; Knight, D. L; Schenider, C. L.; and Smith, P. A. 2001. *Opening Doors: Promising Lessons from Five Texas High Schools.* Austin: The Charles A. Dana Center, University of Texas Austin.

Covey, S. R. 1994. *First Things First.* New York: Fireside.

Duke, D. L. 2011. Building a collaborative culture at South Hills. Unpublished case study.

Duke, D. L. and Jacobson, M. 2011. Tackling the toughest turnaround—low-performing high schools. *Kappan,* 92(5), 34–38.

Finnigan, K. S. and Stewart, T. J. 2009. Leading change under pressure: An examination of principal leadership in low-performing schools. *Journal of School Leadership,* 19(4), 586–618.

Johnson, J. F. and Acera, R. 1999. *Hope for Urban Education: A Study of Nine High-Performing, High-Poverty, Urban Elementary Schools.* Austin: The Charles A. Dana Center, University of Texas Austin.

Picucci, A. C.; Brownson, A.; Kahlert, R.; and Sobel, A. 2002. *Driven to Succeed: High- Performing, High-Poverty, Turnaround Middle Schools.* Austin: The Charles A. Dana Center, University of Texas Austin.

Watkins, M. 2003. *The First 90 Days.* Boston: Harvard Business School Press.

Ensuring Early Progress

A School Turnaround Plan has been developed. Now the task at hand is seeing that the plan is implemented successfully. Remember that many of the strategies associated with successful turnarounds also were tried in turnarounds that failed. What made the difference? Many things, of course, but they all can be traced in one way or another to leadership. Leadership is needed to direct implementation efforts, manage and monitor various components of the School Turnaround Plan, and deal with unforeseen issues that invariably crop up and threaten to sidetrack school improvement.

This chapter is not about a particular plan or collection of turnaround strategies. Instead, the focus involves the steps you will need to take in order to ensure that progress is made, regardless of the specific details of your School Turnaround Plan. The chapter begins with an examination of project management and how it can be used to maintain momentum for improvement. Subsequent sections address the critical role of organizational routines, the benefits of making students part of improvement efforts, and the importance of improving school climate. Sometimes significant improvements are made in the first year of a turnaround initiative, but they do not result in hitting student achievement targets. This should not be cause for despair. Sometimes two years may be needed for a low-performing school to realize achievement gains. The chapter concludes with the story of one such school and how patience and continued hard work paid dividends in the second year of the turnaround process.

THE POWER OF PROJECT MANAGEMENT

It takes a village to raise a child, and it takes a team to turn around a low-performing school. More precisely, it takes a variety of teams. It is often assumed that teachers are targets for improvement in turnaround initiatives. While this is true, it also is the case that teachers are agents of improvement (Cucchiara, Rooney, and Robertson-Kraft, 2013). It is the principal's responsibility to find appropriate structures for focusing teachers' expertise and energy in ways that support collective accountability and creative collaboration. Project management offers such a structure.

Assume that you have developed a 90-day plan to guide the first phase of the school turnaround process. This plan consists of some broad goals, specific objectives associated with each goal, and one or more strategies for accomplishing each objective. A project manager should be assigned to each strategy or, if the strategies are not especially complex, to each objective. A project manager can be an assistant principal, a teacher, a guidance counselor, or some other staff member. It is not a good idea, however, for you, the principal, to be a project manager. Why? Because the principal must be the person to whom project managers report, as will be explained momentarily.

The selection of project managers is one of the most important decisions a principal must make. The fate of the school turnaround process rests with the ability of project managers to execute the strategies called for in the 90-day plan. In order to do so, each project manager is empowered by you to form a project management team. Teams can be made up of various individuals, including administrators (other than the principal), teachers, non-teacher staff members, students, parents, community members, and central office personnel. The makeup of each team depends on the nature of the strategies and the talents needed to implement them.

Take a strategy that calls for home visits to welcome new families to the school. Planning and conducting these visits could be undertaken by a team consisting of a guidance counselor, one or more teachers, perhaps a student who has been at the school for a while, and a translator if necessary. It is probably best, however, if visits are conducted by no more than three team members.

Project managers should be individuals with a track record for being well organized and getting things done. Once they form a team, the team's first task is to develop an Action Plan that specifies what must be done on a week-by-week basis to accomplish its objective. Table 8.1 provides an example of such an Action Plan.

Table 8.1.   Project Management Team Action Plan

Goal (long-term): Raise the percentage of seventh grade students scoring "proficient" on the state reading test to 90 percent.
Objective: Implement "reading across the curriculum" initiative in seventh grade social studies and science classes.
Strategy 1: Use Lesson Study to promote the design of social studies and science lessons that address vocabulary development and reading comprehension.

Completion Date	Activity	Purpose
Week 1	Provide professional development on Lesson Study.	Train all seventh grade social studies and science teachers to implement Lesson Study.
Week 2	Divide into subgroup for social studies and subgroup or science. Observe video of each teacher delivering instruction.	Familiarize group members with each teacher's current instructional process.
Week 3	Each subgroup designs a lesson that addresses reading comprehension and vocabulary as well as required content (based on pacing guide).	Practice lesson design process.
Week 4	Each subgroup chooses a teacher to implement lesson. Lesson is videotaped. Each subgroup meets to view video and critique lesson.	Determine if lesson needs to be adjusted.
Week 5	Each subgroup chooses another teacher to implement the same lesson, including any adjustments. Each subgroup meets to view video and critique lesson.	Determine if lesson is ready to be included in "reading across the curriculum" program.
Week 6	Two subgroups meet to discuss the Lesson Study process and whether to continue designing and testing lessons.	Assess the value of collaborative lesson design.

The project management team in table 8.1 is responsible for implementing Lesson Study as a strategy for promoting a "reading across the curriculum" initiative. Lessons are supposed to address vocabulary development and reading comprehension as well as required academic content for seventh grade social studies and science. This work is one component of a larger effort to increase the percentage of seventh graders scoring proficient on the state reading test.

The team created a six-week Action Plan to test the value of Lesson Study. After receiving training from an instructional coach on the Lesson Study process, the team, which consisted of all seventh grade social studies and science teachers, broke up into two subgroups—one for each subject area. Each subgroup then designed a sample lesson, selected one member to teach the lesson, and arranged to have the lesson videotaped. Each subgroup next reviewed the videotaped lesson, critiqued it, and made adjustments to strengthen the lesson. The process was repeated with another subgroup teacher in order to determine if the lesson accomplished the desired objectives.

By the end of Week 6, the two subgroups were to meet together in order to decide whether Lesson Study was a useful strategy for integrating reading instruction into social studies and science lessons. If they judged the process to be of benefit, the next step would involve creating another Action Plan to expand the initiative.

Turnaround Tip: Implement project management in order to keep staff members focused on high-priority turnaround objectives.

You may be wondering about your role, as principal, in project management. As already noted, your first task is to appoint project managers. Once each project manager has formed a project management team and developed an Action Plan, your job is to review each Action Plan and offer any advice that you feel is called for. Your third responsibility is to form a project management coordinating committee (PMCC) and serve as its chair. This group may include members of your leadership team, grade-level leaders, department chairs, and perhaps district representatives.

The primary purpose of the PMCC is to receive reports every two weeks or so from each project manager on their Action Plan's progress. Regular reporting keeps individuals focused on the objectives of the 90-day plan and enables you to monitor progress closely. Project managers share any concerns that have arisen and ideas for adjusting their Action Plans. The PMCC is not just a monitoring body, however. It is also a source of support, suggestions, and resources. The members of the PMCC should be individuals who can cut through red tape to obtain the approvals and resources required by project managers.

The PMCC periodically may decide that midcourse corrections in the entire School Turnaround Plan are required. No plan is perfect. Sticking with parts of a plan that have proven to be overly ambitious or poorly matched to available resources does not benefit students or staff. As noted earlier, the value of 90-day plans over traditional yearly plans is that changes can be made in time to produce improvements during the current year. Waiting until the following school year to correct problems can place many students at risk, and that is not a price worth paying.

At the end of the first 90-day plan, usually in late November or early December, the PMCC should work with the school leadership team (membership typically overlaps) to evaluate how well the objectives of the plan were met and to develop the next 90-day plan. This follow-up plan extends the work of the prior plan, thereby promoting the idea of continuous planning. In some cases, new project managers will be appointed and new project management teams will be formed. It depends on whether or not additional objectives are included in the new plan.

School Improvement Plans often have been criticized for being forgotten as soon as they are written. Project management coupled with the project management coordinating committee ensure that school personnel remain focused on priority goals and objectives throughout the year.

ORGANIZATIONAL ROUTINES

Low-performing schools desperately need to change; therefore it may sound odd to argue that they also require a large measure of stability. The fact is, however, that successful organizational change actually depends on stability (Kanter, 1991). A study of teachers' working conditions in thirteen schools going through the early stages of the turnaround process found that schools with more favorable working conditions, as perceived by teachers, were characterized by high levels of stability and a clear focus on instruction and climate (Cucchiara, Rooney, and Robertson-Kraft, 2013). Teachers in the schools perceived to have poor working conditions complained that programs and schedules constantly were being changed. They had trouble getting their bearings under these circumstances. No sooner would they adjust to one organizational arrangement than it would be modified or abandoned in favor of a new arrangement.

When everything in a school seems to be changing, it is difficult for teachers to know what to focus on. All sense of priority is lost. As principal, you must make a concerted effort to establish and maintain routines for handling day-to-day operations. Routines contribute to predictability, and predictability is the key to stability. Teachers need to know that they can count on procedures to be followed for such managerial functions as ordering materials, scheduling classes, identifying students in need of help, handling discipline, and assigning space.

In the absence of established routines, individuals are tempted to "do their own thing." When teachers vary greatly in how they conduct classroom and school business, students can be adversely affected. Students are sensitive to and about inconsistencies across classes and within classes. Students raised in poverty often lack structure and predictability at home. Getting a double dose of inconsistency at school is hardly what they need.

When a team of researchers (Spillane, Parise, and Sherer, 2011) looked closely at how four low-performing Chicago K–8 schools responded to demands for greater accountability in the wake of the No Child Left Behind Act, they found that a number of important functions had become routinized. One newly appointed principal, for example, introduced regular grade-level meetings, morning rounds, report-card review, grade-book review, and lesson-plan review. Her objective was to establish a high degree of instructional standardization by implementing these routines. Another principal required teachers to update student skill charts on a regular basis so that student progress could be closely monitored.

To make certain that groundwork is laid for ongoing school improvement, you will need to consider where organizational routines are most needed. Meeting before school each morning with members of your leadership team, for example, can be a very useful routine for discussing the day's responsibilities and any issues that have to be addressed. A similar meeting immediately after school provides an opportunity to debrief and plan for the next day.

Regular occasions for sharing information prevent leadership team members from losing touch with each other and alert them to potential problems.

Scheduling regular meetings with feeder school representatives and local law enforcement officers are other examples of routines that can be of immense value to leaders of low-performing schools. You need to know about issues and concerns in the schools that send students to your school. Maintaining lines of communication with feeder schools can prevent the development of adversarial relations and contribute to greater cooperation across schools. Regular meetings with local law enforcement officers provide occasions for checking on rumors, discussing gang-related activities and other potential safety threats, and coordinating preventive strategies.

Turnaround Tip: Establishing productive organizational routines helps to provide the stability and predictability needed to undertake major school improvements.

Any good idea, of course, can be overdone. Nothing is more upsetting to busy educators than to be subjected to meaningless routines. Every routine—from lesson plan reviews to faculty meetings—should have a clear and credible purpose and some form of follow-up. Your responsibility is to make certain that staff time is not wasted and that routines contribute to the overall turnaround initiative.

STUDENTS ARE ALLIES

Earlier the point was made that teachers are agents of change as well as targets for change. So, too, are students. They have important roles to play in the turnaround process. Several examples already have been shared concerning Nancy Weisskopf's efforts to enlist student support at South Hills High School. Students contributed to rebranding the school, determining the best time to offer after-school academic help and identifying content with which they were struggling. She got the idea for preventing repeaters from taking classes with first timers from students. Students also told her that they did not want single-sex classes in certain subjects, an idea she was considering at the time.

One of the most important steps taken at South Hills to demonstrate the vital role of students in school improvement involved the creation of the Scorpion Student Leadership Council. In many low-performing schools, student councils are either ineffective or nonexistent. Weisskopf believed that students needed an official "voice" and an opportunity to develop leadership skills. One of the responsibilities of the Scorpion Student Leadership Council was to help plan the annual summer boot camp for rising ninth graders.

With all that principals have to do, it is easy to lose touch with students. Much research on principals plays down their ability to have direct effects on students. Instead, principals are seen as indirectly affecting students by working directly with teachers. A group of researchers found, however, that principals also can have a direct effect on student academic achievement (Silva, White, and Yoshida, 2011). Their study examined the impact of one-on-one discussions between a principal and eighth grade students who were struggling with reading. Students who met with their principal before taking the state reading test showed significantly larger reading gains than students who did not meet with their principal. The findings of this study once again underscore the importance of relationship building.

Students also have a role to play when it comes to assessing instructional effectiveness. You may visit a teacher for a formal observation several times a year. You also may conduct periodic walkthroughs just to check on how things are going. Students, however, are in class every day. They are in a better position to comment on a range of instructional factors, including the clarity of teacher directions, the continuity of lessons over time, and the availability of teacher assistance when they get stuck. An excellent source of sample instruments for collecting student perceptions of instruction can be found in Rick Stiggins's *Defensible Teacher Evaluation* (2014, pp.123–125).

Turnaround Tip: Student advice and input is an important part of the school turnaround process.

SCHOOL CLIMATE

It can take years to achieve significant changes in school culture, but that does not mean that quick improvements cannot be made to the daily climate in a low-performing school. Over time, in fact, such improvements can help transform school culture. Mention already has been made of an important focus for climate change—safety and discipline. Nothing undermines school climate more than disorder, disrespect, and disruption. Any steps that you take to address these issues—steps that are considered first-order strategies— can lead to climate improvement. If these steps focus only on more rules and harsher punishments, however, school climate actually may deteriorate.

The best approach to reducing behavior problems involves a balance between fair and consistent enforcement of basic rules and a system of encouragement for positive behavior coupled with relationship building between students and teachers. Like anything else, appropriate behavior is learned. Direct instruction in how to behave in school along with modeling of appropriate conduct and reinforcement when students behave appropriately are important components of any systematic approach to school behavior (Duke, 2002). So, too, are lessons in how to avoid unsafe situations and how to resolve conflict peacefully.

Reducing discipline problems is one route to improving school climate. Another involves efforts to boost the morale of school staff. It is difficult to develop a positive climate for students when teachers and other school personnel feel unappreciated and dissatisfied with working conditions. When it comes to boosting morale, little things can mean a lot. A study of four North Carolina schools that improved enough to exit improvement status found that their principals took a variety of steps to address morale issues (Corcoran, Peck, and Reitzug, 2013). These steps included the following:

- providing teachers with small tokens of appreciation
- organizing fun faculty gatherings
- providing catered breakfasts and lunches during the school year
- providing class coverage when teachers needed a break
- writing notes of appreciation

The same study also found that principals acted to boost student morale as well. They found occasions to celebrate student successes with special assemblies and publicity. They sometimes made "crazy" agreements with students, such as shaving their head if students met a goal. Principals elsewhere have organized pep rallies before students take state tests and initiated community-wide campaigns to reward students for academic success.

A good occasion for celebration is when an objective from the School Turnaround Plan has been achieved. Those involved in achieving the objective, including staff and students, should be recognized, no matter how modest the objective. Any success builds confidence, and confidence leads to further success. Celebrating the achievement of school turnaround objectives also reinforces the value of sticking to a plan and not getting sidetracked. Waiting until the end of the school year to celebrate achieved objectives is unwise because opportunities to sustain momentum and boost school climate along the way are lost.

Generating commitment to a cause that goes beyond one's own self-interest is another way that school climate can be improved. Encouraging students to do well on state tests, not just for their own sake, but for the sake of their school, can be a powerful appeal. Students don't like it when their school scores poorly when compared to other schools. They may be more willing to work hard in order for their school to achieve a higher academic rating than a crosstown rival than they would for their own benefit.

Turnaround Tip: Encouraging students to do well academically for the sake of their school's reputation can be a powerful strategy for improving school climate.

PROGRESS AND PERSISTENCE

Reference to Matt Landahl and his efforts to lead the turnaround process at Greer Elementary School already has been made in an earlier chapter. It is worth going into greater detail about his experience because the story of Greer's turnaround illustrates how progress can be made in the first year without necessarily raising test scores (Duke and Landahl, 2011). By being persistent and making adjustments, however, Landahl and his colleagues were able to make significant student achievement gains by the end of the second year of the turnaround process.

Greer was the most diverse elementary school in Albemarle County, Virginia. Students represented thirty different countries. African American students made up 40 percent of the student body (the county average was 13.5 percent). Approximately half of Greer's students qualified for free or reduced price lunch, and the school's mobility rate was 27 percent, by far the highest in Albemarle County.

Greer's test scores began to slip in 2005–2006. Landahl believed that one reason for this slippage involved the failure of Greer's faculty to make the instructional adjustments required to meet the needs of the school's increasingly diverse student body. Low passing rates on the state's mathematics tests initially kept Greer from meeting accountability requirements under No Child Left Behind. The pass rate for disadvantaged students was 51 percent, while only 43 percent of African American students achieved passing scores.

A greater focus on mathematics resulted in improved pass rates in mathematics the next year, but lower pass rates on the state's English tests prevented Greer from making all of its Adequate Yearly Progress benchmarks once again. Greer consequently entered improvement status, and the Albemarle superintendent decided that a change in leadership was needed in order to effect a turnaround.

By the time Landahl assumed the principalship in late summer, little time was left for planning. Working with his assistant principal, Lisa Molinari, he identified four areas where immediate change was needed. Teachers lacked a clear sense of direction, struggling students needed more effective instruction and assistance, better coordination within and across grade levels was required, and school climate had to be improved.

The focus of efforts to improve instruction would be reading—specifically reading in the upper grades. Conventional thinking might have zeroed in on the lower grades, but Landahl felt that Greer's current group of older students would be at a decided disadvantage in middle school if they did not improve their reading skills. There would be time later on to make improvements in the lower grades' reading program.

The first step in improving reading involved revising the daily schedule in order to increase the time for daily reading instruction to 150 minutes. This meant reducing the time for mathematics to 90 minutes a day. Landahl was aware that mathematics achievement might be adversely affected, but he believed that the possible trade-off was worth it.

At the time Landahl had not heard about project management, but even if he had been aware of the strategy, it is doubtful that he would have implemented it early on. Landahl was unsure that his faculty possessed the leaders capable of managing and monitoring the changes needed to raise student achievement. He elected instead to adopt a highly directive, top-down leadership style.

A primary focus for Landahl's efforts during Year 1 of school turnaround involved the establishment of new and more effective organizational routines. To support the new reading initiative, he instructed teachers to implement ability grouping across classrooms at each upper grade level. So, while stronger readers from various fifth grade classrooms worked with one teacher, weaker readers who needed to focus on comprehension skills went to another teacher's class. Landahl hoped that this move would lead in time to greater cooperation among teachers and a more collaborative school climate as well as higher achievement in reading.

To stay in touch with how the new grouping routine was working, Landahl and Molinari implemented another new routine—learning walks. Every four to six days, they toured classrooms in order to determine how teachers were using the increased time for reading instruction. Based on what they observed, Landahl and Molinari identified instructional improvement goals for each teacher. These goals became the basis for individual professional development plans, another new routine.

The format for professional development plans included "I statements" to help teachers determine if they were making progress. The "I statements" below are examples.

I can hone my skills in using the workshop model to explicitly teach the use of comprehension strategies when reading for multiple purposes.

I can develop quality literacy learning targets for my students in reading and assess them through a variety of informal assessments.

Before Landahl arrived, teachers had gotten out of the habit of meeting regularly to review student progress and plan lessons. Landahl implemented weekly grade-level meetings and vertical meetings across grade levels on a less frequent basis. At least once a month Landahl expected teachers in their grade-level meetings to identify students who needed additional help and areas of the curriculum that posed problems for students. Vertical meetings were devoted to curriculum alignment and discussions of how better to prepare students for the next grade level.

Landahl hoped that grade-level and vertical meetings would improve school climate. He also sensed that there was too much pressure to improve test scores. To balance the emphasis on test-based achievement, he introduced a variety of clubs. Offered after school on Tuesdays in place of tutoring sessions, clubs provided opportunities for students and teacher-sponsors to interact around fun activities. Landahl also reached out to parents in the hopes that they would become more engaged in the school. Parents were invited to a newly established "Heritage Night" where they shared their experiences.

Other steps to improve school climate focused on reducing inappropriate and disruptive student behavior. A consistent set of expectations was developed for conduct in class, at lunch and recess, in the halls, and before and after school. These expectations were communicated and reinforced at schoolwide morning meetings and in classroom gatherings. Alternatives to punishment were developed, and teachers agreed to make a greater effort to recognize students for good behavior.

Funding was obtained to support a two-day faculty retreat at the close of the school year. Landahl saw the retreat as an opportunity to reflect on the first year of the turnaround process and gather faculty suggestions for the next year's plans. At the retreat, teachers expressed their belief that major strides forward had been made in Year 1. Student behavior had improved, teachers were cooperating more, and procedures to identify and help struggling readers had been implemented. Everyone looked forward to getting the results of state testing.

On August 28, 2008, the local newspaper reported the results of state testing. Six Albemarle County schools, including Greer, failed to meet designated benchmarks. Despite the progress made over the previous year, achievement for African American students and disadvantaged students actually dropped slightly. Pass rates for the two subgroups also fell in mathematics. Needless to say, disappointment at Greer was widespread.

Good leaders do not blame others for disappointing results; they take responsibility for them. So it was with Matt Landahl. He admitted that he had spent so much time documenting several weak teachers that he had not focused sufficiently on high priorities in Greer's turnaround plan. Year 2, however, would begin without those teachers. They had been replaced with new teachers who were capable of addressing the needs of Greer's struggling students.

Landahl was optimistic that the new school year would bring improvements in student achievement, and he asked the faculty to rededicate themselves to the turnaround process. A slogan was adopted to capture the mission at hand—"7:45 to 2:25." The implication was clear: if student achievement was to rise, it had to be accomplished between 7:45 a.m. and 2:25 p.m., five days a week.

Landahl and Molinari began to consider the adjustments that would be needed in Year 2. The daily allotment of time for reading and literacy instruction was bumped up from 150 to 245 minutes. Grouping students by ability would continue for basic instruction, but no longer for remediation. Landahl concluded that by fifth grade the same students probably had been in remedial reading groups for many years. Managing these groups was a major problem because the students continually acted out. One-on-one help on a pullout basis replaced the remedial groups.

Another adjustment involved writing instruction. In Year 1 writing had not been stressed in order for teachers to focus more on reading comprehension. Landahl and Molinari now concluded that this had been a mistake. When they consulted research on literacy, they found that writing actually can lead to greater reading comprehension. They subsequently asked teachers to implement a new program that called for daily writing.

To further bolster the reading initiative, Landahl made adjustments in teaching assignments. Now that he had a year of getting into classrooms and observing teachers, he had a clearer sense of who his strongest reading teachers were. Landahl assigned these teachers to instruct the lowest reading groups. To assist them, he also directed his two part-time reading specialists to provide in-class support.

Because Greer was in improvement status, after-school tutoring had to be made available at no charge to students whose parents opted for it. Ten percent of Greer's Title I allocation was earmarked for tutoring. Landahl doubted that high-quality tutoring was being provided by the vendors that parents selected early in the school year. When he observed the after-school tutoring sessions, his fears were confirmed, and he informed state authorities that the Title I funds were being wasted.

Having replaced weak teachers with highly qualified individuals and knowing which teachers were capable of exercising positive leadership,

Landahl appointed new grade-level leaders. He also revived the leadership team, which had been dormant in Year 1 of the turnaround process. With the backing of the new teacher leaders, Landahl reorganized the first grade team, which he regarded as instructionally weak. A new daily schedule also was implemented, thereby enabling teacher teams to meet during the regular school day instead of after school. This change contributed greatly to an improved school climate.

Continuing Year 1 efforts to work on student behavior, Landahl asked teachers if they wanted to expand a pilot program involving Responsive Classroom. Teachers indicated that they liked the program and its emphasis on classroom community building. To support Responsive Classroom, two Success Nights replaced Year 1's Heritage Night. Success Nights became occasions when students shared their work with parents and discussed their academic progress.

August 13, 2009, brought the news the Greer community had waited for. Greer went from being one of Albemarle County's lowest achieving elementary schools to one of the district's top performers. The pass rate in English jumped from 80 to 87 percent, while the mathematics pass rate climbed from 84 to 97 percent. Even more impressive, the pass rate in English for African American students rose from 59 to 85 percent, exceeding the subgroup's pass rate for the district and the state. The mathematics pass rate for African American students climbed from 66 to 93 percent. Similar gains were made for the disadvantaged subgroup. Greer was closing the achievement gap while raising achievement across the board.

It had taken two years to see gains in achievement from Greer's turnaround initiative. Behind these gains was an unwillingness on the part of Matt Landahl to accept defeat after Year 1, the commitment of a large portion of Greer's teachers to keep focused on key priorities in Year 2, and an understanding that any turnaround plan, no matter how well thought out, requires fine tuning and adjustment. Landahl and his colleagues built on the first-order strategies implemented in Year 1, but they also made changes to routines and interventions that had failed to produce desired outcomes. The lesson to be learned echoes a theme throughout this book: leading a low-performing school through the turnaround process depends on regular progress monitoring and continuous planning.

REFERENCES

Corcoran, C.; Peck, C.; and Reitzug, U. C. 2013. Exiting school improvement sanctions. In B. Barnett, A. R. Shoho, and A. J. Bowers (eds.), *School and District Leadership in an Era of Accountability*. Charlotte, NC: Information Age Publishing (IAP), 63–83.

Cucchiara, M. B.; Rooney, E.; and Robertson-Kraft, C. 2013. "I've never seen people work so hard!" Teachers' working conditions in the early stages of school turnaround. *Urban Education, 49*(1), 1–29.

Duke, D. L. 2002. *Creating Safe Schools for All Children*. Boston: Allyn & Bacon.

Duke, D. L. and Landahl, M. 2011. "Raising test scores was the easy part": A case study of the third year of school turnaround. *International Studies in Educational Administration, 39*(3), 91–114.

Kanter, R. M. 1991. Managing the human side of change. In D. A. Kolb, I. M. Rubin, and J. S. Orland (eds.), *The Organizational Behavior Reader*, 5th ed. Englewood Cliffs, NJ: Prentice-Hall, 674–682.

Silva, J. P.; White, G. P.; and Yoshida, R. K. 2011. The direct effects of principal-student discussions on eighth grade students' gains in reading achievement: An experimental study. *Educational Administration Quarterly, 47*(5), 772–793.

Spillane, J. P.; Parise, L. M.; and Sherer, J. Z. 2011. Organizational routines as coupling mechanisms: Policy, school administration, and the technical core. *American Educational Research Journal, 48*(3), 586–619.

Stiggins, R. 2014. *Defensible Teacher Evaluation*. Thousand Oaks, CA: Corwin.

9

Sustaining Progress

There is ample evidence that low-performing schools can make quick and dramatic achievement gains in one to two years (Aladjem et al., 2010; Chenoweth, 2007; Corallo and McDonald, 2002; Duke et al., 2005; Johnson and Acera, 1999; Lane, Unger, and Rhim, 2013). But can these gains be sustained over time? Leaders of low-performing schools continually ask themselves this vexing question. Research has failed to provide a conclusive answer. Several studies offer evidence that some low-performing schools can hold on to gains beyond initial turnaround and even continue to increase student achievement (Bryk et al., 2010; de la Torre et al., 2012; Thompson et al., 2011). Other studies find that examples of schools that sustain early success are outnumbered by those that lose momentum and slip back into academic decline (Hagelskamp and DiStasi, 2012; Huberman et al., 2011; Stuit, 2010).

The mixed findings on sustained improvement in low-performing schools can be interpreted as a glass half full or a glass half empty. It is all up to you. Effective leaders of low-performing schools are optimists. They focus on possibilities rather than probabilities. If Ron Edmonds was still alive, he would remind us that all we need is one turnaround school that sustains early gains in order to demonstrate that it is possible. Knowing that there actually are lots of success stories, we must strive to understand what distinguishes them from the schools that fail to maintain early gains. The key question to ask ourselves, in other words, shifts from "Is it possible to sustain the turnaround of a low-performing school?" to "Why aren't some school turnarounds able to be sustained?" In this regard, it is instructive to return to Greer Elementary School during Year 3 of Matt Landahl's turnaround efforts (Duke and Landahl, 2011).

AN UNFINISHED AGENDA

Recall that impressive achievement gains in English and mathematics had been made in the second year of school turnaround at Greer. African American and disadvantaged subgroups had closed the gap between their pass rates on state tests and those of white students. Pass rates in history and science were a different story, however. Landahl acknowledged that trade-offs had been made. Additional efforts would be needed to boost performance in history and science so that Greer could celebrate across-the-board success.

Because two years of gains in English and mathematics were required under the provisions of No Child Left Behind before a school was allowed to exit improvement status, Landahl faced a key decision for the 2009–2010 school year. Either he had to continue the mandated after-school tutoring program or offer parents the option of enrolling their children in another Albemarle County elementary school. Knowing that the tutoring program was far from effective, Landahl took a risk and notified parents of the transfer option. His gamble paid off. Word of Greer's improved pass rates had spread. Not only did no parents choose the transfer option, but Greer actually picked up twenty-five additional students!

The School Turnaround Plan that Landahl filed with the Virginia Department of Education included ambitious goals for 2009–2010. Pass rates in English would rise from 87 to 95 percent. Mathematics pass rates would inch up from 97 to 97.5 percent. Greer teachers would implement "assessment for learning" strategies in all subjects and for all grade levels. These strategies were intended to encourage academic and character growth through goal setting, reflection, progress tracking by students, and greater personal responsibility. The last goal called for improvements in Greer's professional learning community. Landahl was especially interested in promoting more staff collaboration around issues of safety and discipline.

By his third year at Greer, Landahl felt comfortable distributing leadership more widely among his faculty. Having now hired more than half of Greer's teachers, he knew there was a critical mass of individuals who shared his vision for the school. Teacher-led committees were created to carry out many important functions, including work on the School Turnaround Plan. Committees were formed to address active pedagogy in reading, scheduling, mathematics and technology, communications, community culture, and student culture. Teachers' willingness to assume leadership roles on the committees signaled to Landahl that the Greer culture finally was changing.

Over the course of the 2009–2010 school year, the committees planned and provided various professional development workshops. The scheduling committee rearranged the schedule to allow more time for instructional interventions. Teachers also began conducting peer observations and "instructional rounds." Landahl felt so positive about the faculty that he began encouraging teachers to develop their own professional growth goals. Previously, he had dictated the goals that teachers were to work on.

Work on implementing Responsive Classroom continued, and a new program, Expeditionary Learning, was introduced. Expeditionary Learning endorsed a variety of practices, including student-led conferences, learning expeditions, and the use of portfolios to showcase student progress. Landahl believed that these practices would enhance teaching and learning, thereby extending the successes of Year 2.

Literacy continued to occupy a substantial portion of every school day, but some adjustments were made in Year 3. Students for the first time were grouped *across* grade levels, based on their reading ability. In order to undertake this new initiative, all third, fourth, and fifth grade teachers were scheduled to teach reading at the same time. A similar arrangement was introduced for first and second grade teachers. Landahl believed that cross-age grouping represented a better use of teacher expertise and a more effective way of delivering appropriate instruction.

The nearly three hours a day devoted to literacy was broadened to encompass reading in the content areas of social studies and science. Landahl realized that student achievement in these subjects could not be permitted to slip for a second year. Time continued to be set aside for work on writing as well.

After taking a look at efforts to help struggling students, Landahl moved to reduce pullout assistance that required students to leave their classmates and miss out on mainstream instruction. Specialists providing help to students were encouraged to work within the context of regular classrooms while instruction was going on. After-school tutoring continued in Year 3, but it was provided by Greer teachers, not private providers.

The primary unit for curriculum coordination and planning continued to be the grade-level team (in addition to a Title I team and a special-subjects team), but Landahl decided that two meetings a month should be devoted exclusively to analyzing data on student achievement. The support of district instructional coaches was enlisted to assist grade-level teams with these responsibilities. Landahl and his assistant principal met at midyear with each team to find out which students were having problems and to determine how the new format for team meetings was working.

As spring testing time approached, Landahl felt good about the progress that fourth and fifth graders were making. He was less optimistic about third graders, knowing that they had struggled in first grade. Landahl attributed their problems to a dysfunctional first grade team and teacher inexperience.

When results of state testing were received in late June of 2010, Landahl's fears were confirmed. Pass rates in English and mathematics declined almost 10 percent, due to lower scores by third graders. The good news was that pass rates for fourth and fifth graders continued to improve in English and mathematics. Gains also were made in social studies and science. The low third grade pass rates meant, however, that despite gains elsewhere, Greer would remain in improvement status.

Reflecting on Year 3 of the turnaround process, Landahl noted that he had lost his lead third-grade teacher at the end of Year 2. Two weeks of school in the winter had been lost because of unprecedented snowfall in central Virginia. Furthermore, pass rates for third graders were down across the state. Still, after taking these considerations into account, Landahl did what any good leader would do—he accepted personal responsibility for the disappointing third-grade performance.

A conscious decision had been made to focus on fourth and fifth grades in Years 1 and 2 of the turnaround process at Greer. In hindsight, Landahl realized that efforts in Year 3 to bring third graders up to speed in English and mathematics had fallen short. Landahl also admitted that he had not followed through enough with coaching support for third grade teachers. He knew that some of these teachers were not grasping the details of data-driven instruction. Finally, he acknowledged that focus probably was lost as teachers attempted to implement Expeditionary Learning, cross-age ability grouping in English, and teacher-led committees.

It should be noted that pass rates at Greer rebounded in 2010–2011. Renewed momentum resulted from Landahl's openness to troubleshooting the events of Year 3 and learning from mistakes. The loss of focus was corrected, and adjustments were made in the third grade team.

UNDERSTANDING ACHIEVEMENT STALL AND SLIPPAGE

The experience of Greer Elementary School may not be atypical. A year of remarkable achievement gains is followed by an off year. Turning around a low-performing school sometimes resembles a roller coaster ride. Why this is so is not fully understood. Terms such as "implementation dip" and "reform fatigue" have been used to describe the phenomenon, but they offer no substantive explanation for the up-and-down path to school improvement.

Matt Landahl made an interesting comment when asked to compare Greer's successful second year of turnaround with its disappointing third year. He said, "We focused on the things we knew how to do in Year 2" (Duke and Landahl, 2011, p. 111). His implication was clear. Continued gains in Year 3 required additional expertise, expertise that had not yet been acquired, at least not by third grade teachers.

Landahl's comment echoes an observation by Richard Elmore (2007) after he studied two low-performing schools that had improved and then "gone flat." "Significant gains in performance," he wrote, "are usually followed by periods of flat performance" (p. 248). He went on to explain that teachers and administrators may exhaust their repertoire of ideas for raising achievement during the initial phase of improvement. Without additional skills and knowledge, they lack the capacity to move up to a new level of improvement.

Landahl and Elmore attempted to account for the plateauing of academic achievement. Schools where achievement plateaus are poised for decline. Their observations are worthy of consideration, but they remain conjectures. Fact is, we know much more about why and how schools improve than we do about why and how schools plateau and decline (Duke, 2008). One reason for this lack of knowledge is relatively obvious. Schools that have gone flat or fallen in achievement are reluctant to permit researchers to study them.

Until leaders of low-performing schools have better information about the causes of arrested progress and academic decline, the sustainability of turnarounds will remain in jeopardy. The original causes of a school's low achievement obviously can resurface at any time and undermine continued progress. New problems also may arise to threaten early gains. Drawing on a limited collection of case studies and other research, I developed one possible model of the school decline process (Duke, 2008, p. 63). Figure 9.1 portrays this model.

The model consists of *challenges* to a school's ability to provide a quality education for students, *conditions* associated with failure to respond adequately to these challenges, and *consequences* of failure to respond adequately to challenges.

Three challenges long have been associated with school decline. When difficult economic times result in reductions in resources for schools, teaching and learning can be adversely affected. New government mandates for schools, especially unfunded mandates that raise academic requirements, can contribute to academic problems for schools already struggling to meet existing requirements. Demographic changes that result in unexpected influxes of students with special needs also can pose a challenge for schools.

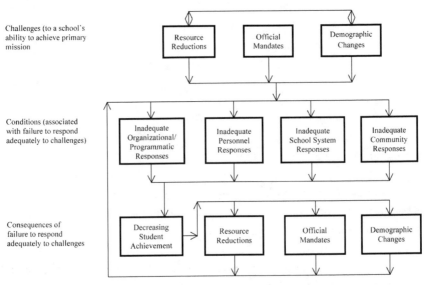

FIGURE 9.1
Model of school decline.

Actual declines in academic achievement, of course, do not result automatically from these challenges. It is the failure of schools to respond effectively to these challenges that contributes to decline. The model in figure 9.1 identifies four areas or conditions associated with inadequate responses. Schools may fail to provide the organizational structures and routines and the academic programs necessary to address challenges. School personnel may not be equipped to handle challenges. Problems at the district level may handicap the ability of schools to respond to challenges. Finally, parents and other community members may be unwilling to support school efforts to respond to challenges.

Any or all of these conditions can lead to declines in student achievement. Lower student achievement, in turn, can lead to additional loss of resources, more official mandates, and further demographic changes. The inability of a school to respond to challenges, in other words, creates a situation in which the school is caught in a downward spiral. Needless to say, escape from such circumstances is extremely difficult.

The three challenges in the previous model derive from developments external to the school. Decline, however, also can result from sources within a school. Many of these sources have been discussed in previous chapters. They range from loss of focus to teacher turnover. Leaders of low-performing schools can do little to prevent loss of resources, new government mandates, and demographic changes, but they can take steps to control school-based factors that threaten the sustainability of gains in student achievement. Among the things that school leaders can attend to in order to sustain improving conditions are the following:

- Adaptive leadership
- Faculty development
- Reculturing
- Curriculum development beyond reading and mathematics
- Community relations
- Troubleshooting

The point that needs to be stressed here is that maintaining the momentum of a turnaround initiative is not just about sustaining gains in student achievement. It also is very much about sustaining capable leadership, faculty growth, an improvement-focused school culture, curriculum adjustment, stakeholder commitment, and measures for anticipating problems before they get out of control. Each of these six keys to long-term success will be examined in the remainder of the chapter.

ADAPTIVE LEADERSHIP

It would be logical to contend that the proper prescription for sustaining achievement gains is to continue doing the things that produced the initial gains. This, however, would be an unwise oversimplification. Continuing effective programs and practices, of course, makes sense, but sustaining success also requires adjustments and fine tuning from time to time. One aspect of the turnaround process that may call for such adjustment and fine tuning is school leadership.

Consider Matt Landahl's experience at Greer Elementary School. He did not feel comfortable distributing leadership to faculty members in his first year at Greer. He was unsure of which teachers he could count on to support the measures that he felt were necessary to raise student achievement. As he got to know his faculty and was able to replace individuals with new hires that embraced his views, Landahl shifted to a less centralized form of leadership. He revived the Leadership Team, made up of grade-level leaders, and eventually devolved considerable responsibility on teacher-led committees.

Research on efforts to sustain school improvement over time consistently underscores the importance of distributed leadership (Copeland, 2003; Johnson and Acera, 1999; Thompson et al., 2011). While newly appointed turnaround principals may start out being highly directive leaders, they probably should not continue to do so. Collective accountability and a collaborative culture are unlikely to develop unless faculty members eventually share in the exercise of leadership.

Sustaining success also may depend on shifting the focus of attention. It is a turnaround principal's primary responsibility to provide direction. To do so entails identifying priorities. If things are working well, the priorities in the third or fourth year of the turnaround process are apt to be different from those in the first and second year. While a shift in focus may be called for, the fact remains—focus is essential. When principals allow routine concerns to become high priorities, focus can be lost and with it the chances of sustaining success.

Maintaining a manageable set of priorities means seeing to it that the School Turnaround Plan continues to be meaningful. Sometimes as low-performing schools improve, the improvement process becomes decoupled from the day-to-day operations of the school. Efforts to continue planning for higher achievement become the business of a small group of staff members, while the rest of the school settles back into their traditional roles and routines. To prevent plans and the planning process from receding into the background, principals of improving schools need to cultivate broad-based teacher ownership in the process. Continuing to employ project management can help.

Generally speaking, the ability of a school to sustain early successes depends on continuity of leadership as well as distributed leadership (Byrne-Jimenez and Orr, 2012). The premature departure of an effective turnaround principal, for example, can have a devastating effect on the improvement process, casting a pall over the school and jeopardizing continued academic gains. There are special circumstances, however, when it is best for a turnaround principal to step aside. Act II leadership can be critical to sustained improvement when the initial turnaround leader is compelled to make unpopular decisions. Such decisions may include cancelling longstanding programs, reallocating resources, and removing or reassigning popular but ineffective staff members. Decisions of these kinds, while important, can undermine the trust so vital to effective leadership.

Succession planning helps to reduce the disruptive effects of a transition in school leadership (Hagelskamp and DiStasi, 2012). It is best for turnaround principals to identify individuals with leadership potential on their staffs and groom them to be potential principal replacements. This means involving them in the planning process and preparing them to function as instructional leaders. Even if they are not eventually chosen to replace the principal, they can provide assistance to whomever is selected and thereby increase the probability of sustained improvement.

FACULTY DEVELOPMENT

Reference to the importance of faculty development already has been made in chapter 5. It is a key not only to school turnaround, but also to the sustainability of early gains in achievement. Developing a faculty capable of addressing the needs of struggling students, in other words, is not a one-time endeavor.

To ensure that school improvements are maintained and expanded, faculty development must be continuous.

As noted in the earlier discussion of first-order strategies, building a capable faculty is multidimensional. It begins with recruitment, selection, placement, induction, and mentoring. Steps then must be taken to ensure that teachers continue to grow. Principals also should not assume that talented teachers will remain on the faculty. Additional measures will be required to retain these teachers.

A newly appointed turnaround principal may not have an opportunity at first to recruit teachers to help launch the turnaround process. In order to sustain success, however, principals will have to work with the human resources department of their school district to develop a recruitment strategy. Such a strategy may involve seeking teachers who reflect the racial, ethnic, and linguistic profile of the student body, who possess the energy and enthusiasm to be good role models, and who have track records of success working with needy students.

Attracting good teachers is one challenge; keeping them is quite another. Teacher turnover rates in schools serving low-income, nonwhite, and low-achieving students can be high—as much as 50 percent higher than in other schools (Ronfeldt, Loeb, and Wyckoff, 2013). A study of the effects of teacher turnover on fourth- and fifth-grade students over an eight-year period in New York City found that student achievement was adversely affected by higher turnover rates, especially in low-performing schools (Ronfeldt, Loeb, and Wyckoff, 2013).

It is not hard to explain high turnover rates in low-performing schools. The work is demanding and often frustrating, and working conditions are frequently difficult. Even in schools engaged in the improvement process, working conditions can be stressful. Yet, there are steps that some principals take in improving schools that lead teachers to perceive working conditions more favorably (Cucchiara, Rooney, and Robertson-Kraft, 2013).

Creating opportunities for teachers to exercise leadership in planning and implementing improvement plans are two important steps that have been mentioned previously. An important component of professional development therefore should be the cultivation of leadership skills in teachers. Matt Landhal understood this and provided guidance and training for his grade-level leaders and committee heads. Delegating authority to capable faculty members is a significant form of recognition and a key step in creating a professional community.

Professional development in other areas besides leadership development also is critical to the sustainability of improvements. Teachers need additional strategies to reach the next level of instructional effectiveness, to refine assessment of student performance, to promote greater academic rigor, and to meet the special needs of students who continue to struggle. Just because some veteran teachers are skilled at helping struggling students is no guarantee that they also are equipped to move students beyond remediation and basic knowledge. Newly hired teachers, on the other hand, need to learn the practices and procedures that experienced teachers already have mastered. Professional development, in other words, must not cease just because students begin to achieve at higher levels, but it should be differentiated based on each teacher's assignment, experience, and effectiveness.

Responsibility for professional development should shift more to the faculty as the turnaround process takes hold. This shift is a significant part of building a professional community and a collaborative culture. There is no reason, for example, why veteran teachers should not play a major role in inducting and mentoring novice teachers.

It is hard to maintain a robust professional community when teacher turnover is high. To reduce turnover, energy must be invested in fostering good working conditions for both new and experienced faculty members. This can mean many things. New teachers, for example, should not be assigned to teach the most challenging students or given large classes and multiple preparations. All teachers appreciate knowing who they can count on and what to expect in terms of support and direction (Cucchiara, Rooney, and Robertson-Kraft, 2013). Ambiguity, inconsistency, and surprises can leave teachers feeling uncertain and uneasy.

Chapter 8 recommended that principals establish organizational routines and open channels of communication. Procedures should be in place for the efficient and consistent handling of everything from disciplinary referrals to purchase orders. Teachers feel disrespected when they do not receive notification of a referral's disposition or they have to wait months to receive classroom materials that they ordered.

Access to the principal also is important to teachers. Turnaround principals who maintained open door policies were regarded much more favorably by teachers than principals who were hard to reach (Cucchiara, Rooney, and Robertson-Kraft, 2013). Finding time during the school day for one-on-one meetings with teachers is one of the most important steps a principal can take to foster positive working conditions, demonstrate that teachers are valued, and sustain the turnaround process.

Turnaround Tip: Positive working conditions for teachers include opportunities to exercise leadership, consistent routines, and open access to the principal.

When principals refrain from taking action to remove weak teachers, they send the wrong message to teachers who are working hard to raise student achievement. Morale is undermined when teachers see colleagues who make little effort to improve, neglect students in need of help, and speak disparagingly of students and fellow teachers. A study of North Carolina schools that exited state sanctions found that principals were quick to identify weak teachers and place them on plans of assistance (Corcoran, Peck, and Reitzug, 2013). Teachers who failed to improve were replaced.

As for effective teachers, principals must make a point of continuing to recognize their contributions. Given all that principals are expected to do, it can be tempting to focus on supporting new teachers and taking veteran teachers for granted. This would be a serious mistake, however, since sustaining the success of a turnaround initiative depends a great deal on the contributions of talented veterans.

RECULTURING

It is not the case that low-performing schools lack an organizational culture. The culture that does exist, however, often is characterized by negative qualities—a willingness to blame others rather than accepting some degree of responsibility for poor achievement, a tendency to criticize first instead of seeking to understand, and reluctance to engage in collective action. New ideas are greeted with skepticism. Needy students are viewed as problems. Parent requests are regarded as intrusive.

Reculturing a school with such a toxic culture takes time, but there are steps that school leaders can take to move the process along. Ignoring school culture is not an option, at least not if the goal is sustained improvement. Principals never should assume that a year or two of promising test results constitutes conclusive evidence of culture change. The cultures of schools that turn around and stay turned around manifest ongoing mission commitment and valuing of continuous improvement, collective accountability, collaboration, coherence, and caring.

Turnaround Tip: Schools that value continuous improvement, collective accountability, collaboration, coherence, and caring are more likely to sustain gains in student achievement.

The mission of every turnaround initiative is to raise student achievement and, with it, the prospects for needy young people. More than lip service must be paid to this mission. The professional staff of low-performing schools have to commit to a continuing effort to improve teaching and learning. When such a commitment becomes an integral part of school culture—when, in other words, people talk about and value improvement and devote significant amounts of time and energy to searching for ways to improve—good things happen. Such a commitment distinguished more successful schools from less successful schools in several studies (Copeland, 2003; Lane, Unger, and Rhim, 2013). It is hard to imagine sustained improvement in schools where faculty members and other stakeholders dismiss reforms as add-ons intended only to accomplish short-term achievement gains in order to avoid sanctions.

Turnaround schools that have recultured also are characterized by a norm of collective accountability (Lane, Unger, and Rhim, 2013). Various kinds of teams, including grade-level teams and student-assistance teams, work together and share responsibility for raising student achievement. Collective accountability and collaboration go hand-in-hand. Instead of competing against each other, teachers join forces, learning from and supporting each other on the journey to higher performance. Eventually, subcultures merge into a unified school culture in which teachers and administrators all pull in the same direction.

Coherence is a by-product of collective accountability and collaboration. Administrators and teachers come to agree on what constitutes good instruction. Vertical articulation characterizes the curriculum. Efforts to assist struggling students are coordinated and timely, not random and disorganized.

Decisions are made for the good of students, not the benefit of particular faculty members or programs.

Perhaps the most indicative characteristic of school cultures poised to sustain improvement is pervasive caring. Teachers care for and about each other as well as their students. Students care for and about each other and their teachers. Such caring entails an awareness of the needs and interests of others (Noddings, 1992). Individual and group differences are met with understanding, not suspicion and criticism. A sense of the common good, rather than narrow self-interest, prevails.

It is easier, of course, to describe a robust school culture than it is to develop one. We are not born with a set of norms. They must be learned, through direct instruction, modeling, trial and error, reinforcement, and sometimes sanctions. Character development does not stop when students leave home to attend school. Educators have roles to play in ensuring that young people learn the norms associated with an effective community of learners. Besides teaching about values such as responsibility and cooperation, teachers make a point of reinforcing students when they manifest these values. Rituals and games are used as occasions to emphasize important norms. Administrators and teachers model caring, respect, and other important values in their daily interactions with each other as well as with students.

CURRICULUM DEVELOPMENT

The early days of school turnaround invariably find teachers focusing on reading and mathematics. This comes as no surprise, since the determination that a school needs to be turned around is based largely on low student achievement in these subjects. Raising achievement in reading and mathematics will launch the turnaround process, but not necessarily keep it afloat. Sustaining gains requires expanding the focus to include other subjects.

Literacy and mathematics for most people are means to various ends—retrieving information, communicating with others, recording thoughts, solving problems, measuring things, and so on. It is in the application of literacy and mathematical skills that students come to realize their value. The ultimate success of a school turnaround should be based on the ability of students to take what they have learned about reading, writing, listening, calculating, measuring, estimating, and predicting, and apply this knowledge to reasoning, understanding, and problem solving in various disciplines and endeavors.

Successful turnaround principals like Nancy Weisskopf discovered that creating high interest courses and majors in fields like computer gaming is critical to student motivation. Student motivation, in turn, is a key to sustained academic progress. Some forward-thinking school systems, recognizing the critical importance of student motivation, have established academies in their high schools. Academies offer students opportunities to spend part of the day focusing on career-oriented learning and applying academic knowledge to the solution of real-world challenges. Students in a building and design academy might plan and construct an actual residence over the course of one or two years, while students in a health care academy work in medical settings supporting the efforts of nurses and physicians.

As states transition to Common Core Standards or comparable sets of rigorous curriculum targets, the importance of applied learning, problem solving, critical thinking, and artistic expression will only increase. Schools that continue to concentrate solely on basic skills risk placing their students at a decided disadvantage.

Turnaround Tip: Sustained progress depends on moving beyond reading and mathematics to engage students in problem solving and other forms of applied learning.

A strong extracurricular program also can be a key to sustained success. I have known turnaround principals who sought to involve every single student in at least one extracurricular activity. Participation in sports, music groups, dance teams, clubs, and other activities motivates students to keep up with their academic work and ensures they remain connected to their school. Teachers who coach and sponsor extracurricular activities often are able to build special relationships with students that serve as important deterrents to giving up and dropping out. Attendance at athletic events, plays, recitals, and other performances also helps to keep parents and community members connected to school.

COMMUNITY RELATIONS

Parent and community interest often is great at the beginning of the turn-around process. Over time, however, as trust between home and school builds and student achievement starts to improve, parent and community involvement may wane. Principals should anticipate this possibility and invest energy in developing a robust parent-teacher organization and partnerships with community organizations. Parents and community members play critical roles as school advocates, especially at times when budget cuts threaten to reverse turnaround gains. They also have vital roles to play as school volunteers and sources of input for improvement planning.

Turnaround Tip: Continuing parent and community involvement is a key to sustained school success.

There is no universal strategy for getting and keeping parents involved. Sometimes the best approach is to work with students to engage their parents and guardians. In other cases, appealing directly to parents and guardians is the preferred course to take. General appeals for involvement tend to be less effective than requests for specific types of participation, such as volunteering to listen to students as they read or attending student-led conferences.

Principals who succeed in developing powerful home-school connections never lose sight of parent concerns. Parents want to know that their children will be safe at school, treated fairly and with respect. They want to be assured that their children are making progress and are on track to graduate. When their children are not making progress, they expect to be informed in a timely manner and learn what steps are being taken to help. Parents also want schooling to be a meaningful and enjoyable experience.

In order to provide the assurances that parents seek for their children, principals need access to resources. Just as a rocket needs extra fuel to achieve lift-off and escape the Earth's gravity, so a low-performing school needs additional resources to reverse years of declining achievement and then maintain gains. Districts with large numbers of low-performing schools often find it difficult to continue funding particular schools at a higher level when many other schools need to be turned around. Special funding through School

Improvement Grants and foundation gifts eventually run out. To ensure that additional resources continue to be available to sustain progress, partnerships with parent and community organizations should be developed and nurtured.

A perfect example of a partnership that has helped to sustain a school turnaround is the partnership between Robert A. Taft Information Technology High School in Cincinnati, Ohio, and Cincinnati Bell (Hagelskamp and DiStasi, 2012). Once regarded as an unsafe "dropout factory," Taft developed a career-oriented academic program focused on information technology. Cincinnati Bell underwrote the program in two ways: (1) an extensive tutoring and mentoring program, and (2) ample incentives to motivate student achievement. Taft students' scores on state tests in reading and mathematics now exceed those for other Cincinnati schools.

Cincinnati Bell tutors make a two-year commitment to help students pass the Ohio Graduation Test. The strengths of tutors are matched with the specific academic needs of individual students. Cincinnati Bell runs a bus from its offices to Taft twice a week so that tutors can meet with students. Incentives to encourage students to work hard range from cellphones and laptops to gift cards. To earn these generous incentives, students must maintain a high grade point average. Ten students a year are awarded $20,000 scholarships to college.

Plenty of low-performing schools have forged partnerships, only to see these arrangements eventually fall by the wayside. To maintain productive partnerships, principals need to keep in close communication with partners, letting them know how their contributions are being used and to what effect. Partners want to know that their investments in education are not being wasted.

TROUBLESHOOTING

Just because a low-performing school arrests academic decline and begins to improve does not mean that problems disappear. Problems are endemic to schools. The difference between sustained improvement and a return to low performance sometimes boils down to recognizing problems early enough to address them effectively—before they become crises. This capacity is referred to as *troubleshooting*.

Veteran principals learn that certain circumstances can be counted on to generate problems. Among these circumstances are changes in personnel and new staffing arrangements. When new staff are hired or existing staff members are moved to new assignments, principals should be alert for possible problems. Individuals may be uncertain about what they are expected to do or unprepared to handle their new duties. Such problems need to be handled quickly before student and staff morale are adversely affected. Other problems may arise when team members are changed or departments are combined to form new units. Being sensitive to the impact of change on staff members is essential to troubleshooting.

New policies and regulations are additional sources of problems. Educators, like most human beings, are creatures of routine. Any change that threatens to upset these routines is likely to be greeted, at least initially, with suspicion and resistance. Ignoring the concerns of those who must implement new policies and regulations leads to frustration, anger, and diminished performance. Principals should make a point of listening to the concerns of staff members and finding mutually acceptable ways of addressing them.

On occasion redistricting or an influx of new families can result in significant enrollment changes. Class sizes may grow, and teachers may be faced with the challenge of teaching students whose cultures and characteristics are unfamiliar. Such circumstances also can be expected to produce problems as teachers struggle to address new demands. Anticipating problems and providing appropriate professional development and other forms of support can prevent enrollment changes from causing major disruptions to teaching and learning.

Mention already has been made of problems associated with transitions from one school to another. Moving from elementary to middle school and from middle to high school often occasion adjustment problems. Ignoring these adjustment problems is an invitation to serious academic and socioemotional concerns. Anyone who doubts this warning should read Camille Farrington's (2014) sobering account of fourteen inner city students and their struggles to survive the first years of high school.

Even success can be an occasion for troubleshooting. A year or two of achievement gains sometimes cause teachers to ease up on improvement efforts. Effective turnaround principals understand that the best defense against backsliding is a commitment to continuous improvement by all staff members. They watch out for indications of easing up, such as relaxed expectations for students and diminished interest in professional development and bell-to-bell instruction.

The British National Audit Office (Comptroller and Auditor General, 2006) investigated keys to sustaining improved student achievement following successful school turnarounds. One of the most frequently noted characteristics of schools that continued to improve was the presence of a culture of self-evaluation. Teachers and administrators did not back off from examining school programs, student progress, and their own actions.

Imagine that a particular school program—say a program to help students struggling with Algebra—is not working. Given how pressed educators are for time, it may seem that the best course of action is to search for a new program. In a culture of self-evaluation, however, the first step would be to examine *why* the current program failed to help students with Algebra. Quickly moving on to a new program without troubleshooting the former program's problems simply may hasten another round of disappointing results.

Senge (1990) ties the downfall of many organizations to their failure to learn from mistakes. No organization is perfect. Poor decisions and missteps will be made. The trouble is that individuals who make the poor decisions and take the wrong steps often do not experience directly the consequences of their actions. A principal makes a unilateral decision to adopt a new school schedule, but he is not the teacher who must hold students' interest for ninety minutes instead of forty-five, nor is he the student who grows impatient with prolonged seatwork. A true *learning organization*, according to Senge, develops mechanisms for continuously reviewing and evaluating decisions and their consequences. The diagnostic questions in chapter 3 can serve as a useful guide for ongoing troubleshooting efforts.

Sustaining early gains from turnaround initiatives clearly is a challenge. Troubleshooting is important, as are adaptive leadership, faculty development, school reculturing, curriculum development beyond reading and mathematics, and community relations. There is one more piece to the puzzle of sustainability, however, and it may be the most critical of all. The last chapter looks at the central role of the school district in supporting and sustaining school turnarounds.

REFERENCES

Aladjem, D. K.; Birman, B. F.; Orland, M.; Harr-Robins, J.; Heredia, A.; Parrish,
T. B.; and Ruffini, S. J. 2010. *Achieving Dramatic School Improvement: An
Exploratory Study.* Washington, DC: U.S. Department of Education.

Bryk, A. S.; Sebring, P. B.; Allensworth, E.; Luppescu, S.; and Easton, J. Q. 2010.
Organizing Schools for Improvement. Chicago: University of Chicago Press.

Byrne-Jimenez, M. and Orr, M. T. 2012. Thinking in three dimensions: Leadership
for capacity building, sustainability, and succession. *Journal of Cases in
Educational Leadership*, 15(3), 33–46.

Chenoweth, K. 2007. *It's Being Done: Academic Success in Unexpected Schools.*
Cambridge MA: Harvard Education Press.

Comptroller and Auditor General. 2006. *Improving Poorly Performing Schools in
England.* London: National Audit Office, Department for Education and Skills.

Copeland, M. A. 2003. Leadership of inquiry: Building and sustaining capacity for
school improvement. *Educational Evaluation and Policy Analysis*, 25(4), 375–395.

Corallo, D. and McDonald, D. H. 2002. What works with low-performing schools:
A review of research. Charleston, WV: Appalachian Regional Educational
Laboratory.

Corcoran, C.; Peck, C.; and Reitzug, U. C. 2013. Exiting school improvement
sanctions. In B. Barnett, A. R. Shoho, and A. J. Bowers (eds.), *School and
District Leadership in an Era of Accountability.* Charlotte, NC: Information Age
Publishing (IAP), 63–83.

Cucchiara, M. B.; Rooney, E.; and Robertson-Kraft, C. 2013. "I've never seen
people work so hard!" Teachers' working conditions in the early stages of school
turnaround. *Urban Education*, 49(1), 1–29.

de la Torre, M.; Allensworth, E.; Jagesic, S.; Sebastian, J.; and Salmonowicz, M. 2012.
Turning Around Low-Performing Schools in Chicago. Chicago: Consortium for
Chicago School Research, University of Chicago.

Duke, D. L. 2008. Understanding school decline. *International Studies in
Educational Administration*, 36(2), 46–65.

Duke, D. L. and Landahl, M. 2011. "Raising test scores was the easy part": A case
study of the third year of school turnaround. *International Studies in Educational
Administration*, 39(3), 91–114.

Duke, D. L.; Tucker, P. D.; Belcher, M.; Crews, D.; Harrison-Coleman, J.; Higgins, J.; Lanphear, L.; Marshall, M.; Reasor, H.; Richardson, S.; Rose, M.; Salmonowicz, M. J.; Scott, W.; Taylor, R.; Thomas, C.; and West, J. 2005. *Lift-Off: Launching the School Turnaround Process in 10 Virginia Schools.* Charlottesville, VA: Darden/Curry Partnership for Leaders in Education, University of Virginia.

Elmore, R. F. 2007. *School Reform from the Inside Out.* Cambridge, MA: Harvard Education Press.

Farrington, Camille. 2014. *Failing at School.* New York: Teachers College Press.

Hagelskamp, C. and DiStasi, C. 2012. *Failure Is Not an Option.* New York: Public Agenda.

Huberman, M.; Parrish, T.; Hannan, S.; Arellanes, M.; and Shambaugh, L. 2011. *Turnaround Schools in California: Who Are They and What Strategies Do They Use?* San Francisco, CA: WestEd.

J. F. and Acera, R. 1999. *Hope for Urban Education: A Study of Nine High-Performing, High-Poverty, Urban Elementary Schools.* Austin: The Charles A. Dana Center, University of Texas Austin.

Lane, B.; Unger, C.; and Rhim, L. M. 2013. *Emerging and Sustaining Practices for School Turnaround.* Baltimore, MD: Institute for Strategic Leadership and Learning.

Noddings, N. 1992. *The Challenge to Care in Schools: An Alternative Approach to Education.* New York: Teachers College Press.

Ronfeldt, M.; Loeb, S.; and Wyckoff, J. 2013. How teacher turnover harms student achievement. *American Educational Research Journal*, 50(1), 4–36.

Senge, P. M. 1990. *The Fifth Discipline.* New York: Doubleday Currency.

Stuit, D. A. 2010. *Are Bad Schools Immortal?* Washington, DC: Thomas B. Fordham Institute.

Thompson, C. L.; Brown, K. M.; Townsend, L. W.; Henry, G. T.; and Fortner, C. K. 2011. *Turning Around North Carolina's Lowest Achieving Schools (2006–2010).* Chapel Hill, NC: Consortium for Educational Research and Evaluation—North Carolina.

10

The Role of the School District in Turnaround Success

Up to this point emphasis has been placed on the critical role of school leaders in turning around low-performing schools. Without capable district leadership, however, even the best efforts of the most dynamic and talented school leaders may be short-lived. Sustaining improvements in student achievement requires a coordinated approach involving *both* school and district leaders. This concluding chapter presents some of the important ways in which district leaders can support school-based turnarounds. The experience of one visionary superintendent and her efforts to turn around an entire school system provides a good starting place.

RICHMOND BUILDS A FOUNDATION FOR SCHOOL SUCCESS[1]
Deborah Jewell-Sherman had no illusions about the challenges facing her in 2002 when she was sworn in as Richmond's seventh superintendent in fourteen years. She had come to Richmond, Virginia, at the behest of Patricia Conn, a fellow doctoral student in Harvard's Urban Superintendents Program and superintendent of Richmond Public Schools from July of 1995 to March of 1997. Conn hired Jewell-Sherman to serve as associate superintendent for community engagement, a post that enabled her to learn a great deal about the public's concerns for its schools. Under Conn's successor, Albert Williams, Jewell-Sherman was moved to associate superintendent for accountability and instruction. In this role she came face-to-face with the school system's dismal track record.

Only one of Virginia's school divisions had a lower level of student achievement than Richmond Public Schools. Of Richmond's fifty-five schools, just five had attained full accreditation status in the fall of 2001 under Virginia's new educational accountability system. Full accreditation meant that at least 70 percent of a school's students passed the state's Standards of Learning (SOL) tests. The tests were administered in the third, fifth, and eighth grades as well as in selected subjects in high school. Twenty-nine Richmond schools were in the lowest category—accredited with warning—which indicated that their passing rates on SOL tests fell twenty or more percentage points below the 70 percent benchmark.

Low passing rates, however, were just the tip of the academic iceberg for Richmond Public Schools and its nearly 27,000 students. The school system's dropout rate (2.7 percent a year) and truancy rate (22 percent) were among the highest in the state. High school students took few advanced courses and scored poorly on the Scholastic Aptitude Tests (SAT). Some observers attributed these problems to Richmond's deteriorating school facilities, perennial financial difficulties, and problems with school violence. School principals recorded 10,961 disciplinary actions, including almost 9,000 suspensions, in 2001–2002. Others blamed teachers for inadequate instruction and low expectations for students. Still others pointed to the low level of parental involvement. Local politics and in-fighting among School Board members also were mentioned as reasons for the school division's lackluster performance.

One matter on which School Board members agreed was the need for a performance-based contract for Deborah Jewell-Sherman. Believed to be the first such contract in Virginia, Jewell-Sherman's two year, eleven-month agreement tied her job security to student performance on state SOL tests. Three conditions had to be met or else she could be fired the following summer: (1) based on spring testing in 2003, at least twenty of Richmond's fifty-five schools had to be fully accredited; (2) no more than twelve schools could be accredited with warning; and (3) at least sixteen of the city's elementary schools had to achieve passing rates of 70 percent or higher on the third grade SOL reading test. At the time she signed the contract, only three schools had attained this benchmark.

Other candidates for superintendent might have shied away from such a contract, but not Deborah Jewell-Sherman. She embraced the agreement and the sense of urgency it represented. At Harvard she had studied urban school systems that managed to improve despite the odds. Having spent time in Tidewater Virginia as a principal, she also was aware that Norfolk, Richmond's sister city, was making impressive strides with a school population similar to Richmond's. As associate superintendent, she already had taken steps to raise student achievement. These steps included implementing the Voyager reading program in summer school and experimenting with a commercial benchmark testing service to track student progress on the state Standards of Learning.

Jewell-Sherman understood that raising student achievement was job one, and she clearly was committed to that aim. No sooner had she moved into her spacious office on the seventeenth floor of City Hall, however, than she was confronted with a series of issues that seemed peripheral to her priorities. She wondered whether she would be able to deal effectively with these issues and still maintain a laser-like focus on improved teaching and learning.

One of the first issues involved the School Board's decision to extend the residential zone within which students were expected to walk to school. The move, intended to reduce the costs of bus transportation, produced a torrent of complaints from parents worried about the safety of their children. Resolving the transportation issue took several months.

Late October brought panic regarding the possible presence of the Washington, DC-area sniper in the vicinity of Richmond. Schools were closed as a precautionary measure. Then, in early November a report on the poor conditions of Richmond's schools by a local architectural firm indicated that as many as fourteen of the city's schools might need to be closed in the coming years. The price tag for renovation and replacement of facilities was set at 350 million dollars. Some of the schools targeted for closure were among Richmond's most revered.

Raising revenue for capital improvements seemed a remote possibility in December when Governor Mark Warner announced that Virginia faced a 1.1 billion dollar revenue shortfall. The timing could not have been worse for Deborah Jewell-Sherman and Richmond Public Schools. She had just presented her funding priorities to a delegation of Virginia legislators. These included more money for literacy programs, alternative education programs, teacher salaries, and school-based police officers. With state funds in short supply, Jewell-Sherman knew that she had nowhere else to turn except the city. This would be the third year in a row that the school division had to beg for increased local funding. Without adequate funding, however, a school division turnaround was unlikely.

January and February found Jewell-Sherman and the School Board grappling with how to cut the budget. Ideas ranged from school closings to curtailing the division's early retirement incentive program. Nearly 12 percent of the budget was spent on employee health care, and almost one-third of this amount was spent on retirees. In the midst of the debates over the budget, the school division received a strongly worded report on its special education program from the state Department of Education. The report indicated that many children who were eligible for special education services, especially those transferring into Richmond schools, were not receiving services. March 21 was set as the date by which a plan for how the problem would be corrected had to be submitted to the state. Few doubted that such a plan would entail increased expenditures at a time when ways to trim the budget were being sought. Not surprisingly the head of Richmond's special education department tendered her resignation in early March.

On March 27, Jewell-Sherman and the School Board learned that its efforts to reduce the budget were not sufficient for City Council. Several council members expressed concern that administrative costs for the school division were increasing while student enrollment was declining. They pointed to other city school systems that operated more efficiently than Richmond.

On June 2, City Council finally approved its allocation to Richmond Public Schools. The figure represented 3.2 million dollars less than had been requested, but it was enough to permit a modest increase in teacher salaries and to enable Jewell-Sherman to move forward with turnaround plans for the lowest achieving schools.

Reflecting on her first year as superintendent, Deborah Jewell-Sherman expressed pride that she had been able to maintain a focus on improved teaching and learning despite the variety of other issues that she and the school system had faced. In order to stick to her commitment, she had enlisted the support of key School Board members, community partners, and central office administrators. Turning around a school system, she realized, was not a solo undertaking.

Unlike some of her fellow superintendents of low-performing school systems, one thing Jewell-Sherman did not do was start off by dismissing principals of schools where student achievement was especially low. She explained her approach as follows:

> The principals never had received the training they needed to be effective. So we trained them to understand data, to use data to lead their staff. But I don't believe in just working with principals. I believe in working with a school's entire leadership team. We work really hard at getting information out to a team—empower the principal to lead, but to lead an instructional or leadership team at the school.

Jewell-Sherman did make one key personnel move, however. She promoted Dr. Yvonne Brandon to her former position of associate superintendent of accountability and instruction. Brandon had been a successful principal and director of instruction and she had a solid grasp of curriculum and instruction. When Jewell-Sherman and Brandon reflected on where to begin district-wide improvements, they both agreed that site-based management, where key decisions regarding curriculum and instruction were left to the discretion of each principal, was not serving the needs of the system. Brandon put it thusly:

> We were working hard, but we weren't working hard on the right things. We had an extremely dedicated staff of teachers, instructional staff, principals, but we did not have a clear definition of how to connect the pieces. We had no centralized curriculum alignment. We did not have any means of assessing our children to determine where they were and what they needed to do to get to the next level. The first step that we took was to look at an inventory of reading and mathematics products throughout the schools. We had previously been experimenting with site-based management. As a result, instruction became very, very varied. Each principal did what they wanted—it was varied in intensity and in product, which didn't quite match with having a 44 percent mobility rate.

Richmond students frequently moved around from one city school to another. To assure that no student was placed at a disadvantage based on his or her school assignment, site-based management would have to give way to greater centralization of decision making regarding curriculum content, instructional methods, and assessment practices. Jewell-Sherman and Brandon knew, of course, that centralization was likely to provoke resistance from school administrators and teachers, but they also understood that system-wide improvements in student achievement were unlikely without such a drastic change.

When Brandon inventoried reading programs in use in Richmond schools, she found elements of twenty-nine different programs. Not only was program consistency from school to school lacking, but often there was no consistency from grade to grade in the same school. Vendors persuaded principals to use their reading programs without offering convincing proof of program effectiveness. Brandon had no intention of continuing this practice.

> So one of the things that we started to do was to research products. We developed a list of critical criteria that a product must have, which included being scientifically based, having embedded assessments, having continuous professional development, and having provisions for training central office and lead administrative staff on a regular basis so that we could monitor the implementation and use of the product. Fidelity to implementation was a big, big issue because, of course, teachers are sometimes territorial. So, when the classroom door was shut, we had to be sure that what needed to be taught was being taught.

Jewell-Sherman's and Brandon's focus on inventorying and assessing reading and mathematics programs in their first year was a major accomplishment, but they did not stop there. They had been in Richmond long enough to know that curriculum inconsistency was only one of many problems. Instructional practice also was inconsistent. What was required, they believed, was a common instructional model for all teachers. Once again, they knew they would encounter resistance, but they realized that curriculum consistency without quality instruction was unlikely to raise student achievement. After extensive research and consultation, a cogent model of instruction emerged and was mandated for the entire school system. Brandon described the model as follows:

> The model follows some of the more respected instructional strategies. You have a snapshot in the beginning of the class. You do direct instruction based on the children's level of understanding. You give guided practice. You give homework. You take the children through some of the steps of the homework.

You give them an opportunity to ask questions. And then you do a maintenance moment to conclude the lesson. That's a question that ties the current
instruction to previous learning.

Jewell-Sherman and Brandon recognized that they needed to address one
more area of concern in order to launch a system-wide effort to raise student
achievement. Many Richmond teachers possessed only a limited knowledge
of Virginia's Standards of Learning. Without a clear understanding of these
standards, teachers were at a disadvantage when it came to preparing their
students to take state standardized tests. Passage of these tests governed pro-
motion and eventual graduation.

Brandon realized that the school system could accomplish two goals if
model lessons were developed for every standard in the state's Standards of
Learning. The task was enormous, but if each model lesson was based on
the newly developed instructional model, then teachers who used the lessons would gain practice with the instructional model at the same time that
they were focusing instruction on the required state standards. Developing
the model lessons also provided an opportunity for classroom teachers to
become directly involved in the process of turning around the school system.
Teachers were paid stipends to work with instructional specialists on lesson
development. Brandon described the process as follows:

> Lesson plans for each SOL include a breakdown of the objective—spiraling
> objectives. And those were objectives that perhaps were taught in the previous
> grade that were related to this objective. We have vocabulary terms, technology
> integration such as Web sites that the teacher could go to. We have field trips
> that were related to SOL objectives. We have critical terms that the teacher
> needed to concentrate on. Basically we created a well-organized book of lesson
> plans for each SOL objective in each subject, K–12.

Looking back on the work accomplished during the 2002–2003 school
year, Jewell-Sherman and Brandon could not help but feel a great deal of
satisfaction. Crucial steps toward curriculum alignment and instructional improvement had been taken. Still, any feelings of satisfaction had to be mixed
with anxiety. Much of the first year's work focused on research and development. The stage clearly had been set for a turnaround, but would the actors
be able to perform?

A SCHOOL SYSTEM MOVES FORWARD

Fast forward to the fall of 2007. The results of the 2006–2007 state tests were in. Tears welled up in Deborah Jewell-Sherman's eyes as she reviewed the data for one of her target turnaround schools. For the third year in a row, Fairfield Court Elementary School had achieved full state accreditation and met Adequate Yearly Progress benchmarks under the No Child Left Behind Act. The school's passing rates—98 percent in third and fifth grade English, 99 percent in mathematics, 100 percent in third grade history, 100 percent in science—placed it among the top-performing elementary schools in Virginia. What made the accomplishment so remarkable was the fact that Fairfield Court Elementary School was located in a public housing project. Ninety-six percent of its students qualified for free lunch. Jewell-Sherman wasn't certain whether her emotional reaction represented tears of relief or tears of joy. One thing, however, was certain—the students and teachers at Fairfield Court had demonstrated that poverty was no excuse for low academic expectations.

While Fairfield Court's record of achievement was impressive, it was not unique. By the 2004–2005 school year, thirty-nine of Richmond's fifty-one schools had been fully accredited by the state. The following year, forty-two of forty-nine schools, or 86 percent of the city's schools, attained full accreditation. The turnaround of Richmond Public Schools had been achieved to a degree sufficient for the state Board of Education in March of 2007 to release the school system from a state review process required of low-performing school systems.

How had Jewell-Sherman and Brandon been able to effect such an impressive turnaround in just five years? The short answer is that they were willing to lead. Jewell-Sherman and Brandon were veteran leaders, and they understood that mandating change from the central office was not without risk. Brandon already had needed to leave her sick bed to appear before the School Board when a small group of angry teachers challenged her efforts to require a common instructional model. Principals had voiced their concerns over the loss of discretionary authority regarding curriculum and professional development. Brandon was not surprised by these reactions. Instead, she took a somewhat philosophical position, maintaining that "it is easier to loosen up than tighten up." If student achievement improved, then principals and teachers should be accorded greater autonomy. If.

When Brandon analyzed student achievement data, it was clear that reading and literacy needed to be addressed first. Gains in other subjects were contingent, to some degree, on improvements in students' ability to comprehend written material, master vocabulary, and communicate effectively, both orally and in writing. Brandon recalled the decision to go with the Voyager reading program in all low-performing schools:

> We had used Voyager products in summer school. We understood that some of our children needed to have intense assessments very quickly and a response from the instructor at the same level of urgency. That's what attracted us to Voyager. And we saw how our children got excited during the summer with the Voyager materials. But then they went back to the normal school program in the fall and had the same "4 across, 5 in a row" kind of classroom arrangement. And the teachers weren't able to do flexible reading groups. When they did what they thought were flexible reading groups, kids were stuck in the same group all year! You had the redbirds, the bluebirds, and the buzzards, just like when I was in school. That doesn't work for children. They need to be able to mingle into groups, move in and out, work with their peers, have concrete content, but have the instruction of that content differentiated. And Voyager allows this. We started out by piloting Voyager, then we looked at the results and saw that it was working. We didn't go full-district, though. What we did was use Voyager for our very lowest performing schools.

Sensitive to commercial providers who sold expensive programs to school systems and then vanished, Jewell-Sherman insisted that Voyager become an active "partner" with Richmond Public Schools. Such a relationship required a commitment on the publisher's part to engage in continued training of teachers and monitoring of program progress. Richmond also implemented a diagnostic testing program linked to the reading program in order to provide teachers with continuous data on how students were performing. Diagnostic and benchmark testing became a hallmark of Richmond's prescription for improved student achievement.

Another hallmark was timely and targeted intervention for students needing assistance. Regular testing tied to the state Standards of Learning provided teachers with the data they needed to pinpoint areas where individual students were struggling. Prompt assistance then could be provided, thereby reducing the possible adverse cumulative impact of delayed help. To provide additional time for learning and remediation, Jewell-Sherman eliminated early release Wednesdays for elementary students. By adding more than two hours of instruction per week, twelve more days of instruction a year were created.

In another move designed to expand learning opportunities, Jewell-Sherman and Brandon got the School Board to approve Twilight School. Brandon described the new venture as follows:

> Twilight School runs from 2:00 to 4:30 p.m. It is an opportunity for students to take either a make-up semester or a full-year course in the afternoons. We run it from Monday through Thursday, getting enough seat hours to satisfy state requirements. Students are provided with small-group instruction. They do one course at a time.

Special education received special attention from the outset of the new administration. Unwilling to leave critical decisions to the faculty and administration of each school, Jewell-Sherman insisted on a system-wide change in approach. As Brandon described it,

> We stopped dealing with special education students in a separate mode. We blended our efforts by having our special education specialists train with our content specialists so they could get a better handle on content versus compliance and regulations. We stopped thinking of special education children as a separate group of children in Richmond Public Schools. All of our efforts were toward training all of the teachers, whether special education teachers or non–special education teachers. And I think it helped because the special ed teachers could no longer say that something was the academic teacher's issue. It became every teacher's responsibility to teach.

To ensure that school principals acquired the skills they needed to implement improvement initiatives, Jewell-Sherman and Brandon saw to it that a professional development program was provided for them. One component of this program involved a partnership with the University of Virginia's new School Turnaround Specialist Program. As principals demonstrated their effectiveness in directing instructional improvement and monitoring student progress, they were granted increased amounts of discretionary authority. Jewell-Sherman and Brandon understood that sustained success ultimately depended on developing the capacity of each school to take charge of its improvement process.

The story of Richmond Public Schools under the leadership of Deborah Jewell-Sherman and Yvonne Brandon contains most of the key elements of school district support for school turnaround. These elements include the following:

1. Top-level leadership for school turnaround initiatives
2. Development of capable school leaders
3. Assistance with school staffing and faculty development
4. Technical support and supplementary resources
5. Restructuring to facilitate district support services

The remainder of this chapter examines each of these key elements.

TURNAROUND BEGINS AT THE TOP

So far this book has stressed the critical role of school-level leadership in raising student achievement. Schools, however, exist within larger organizational entities. Without capable and committed school district leadership, the hard work of principals and other school-based leaders may be for naught.

Maintaining a laser-like focus on turning around low-performing schools may not seem like a great challenge for superintendents and school boards, but anyone who has been in a district leadership position understands how easy it is to lose focus. Distractions abound. Recall Deborah Jewell-Sherman's early days as superintendent of Richmond Public Schools. She faced transportation issues, a sniper crisis, deteriorating facilities, and a serious state budget shortfall. Jewell-Sherman, however, never lost her focus on raising student achievement in low-performing schools. When other matters required her immediate attention, she made certain that Yvonne Brandon, her second-in-command, continued to move the school turnaround agenda forward.

Leading the school turnaround process from the central office can be manifested in manifold ways. Generating a sense of urgency regarding academic improvement. Working to build school board consensus on extra resources for low-performing schools. Steering a course through competing priorities. Recognizing and rewarding success. Waiting for things to happen, though, is one thing that leading is not. Leading is all about taking initiative and providing direction.

When Education Resource Strategies, a nonprofit group, held a Turn-around Summit for central office leaders and principals, it learned about the many facets of central office leadership in the turnaround process (*Sustaining School Turnaround at Scale*, 2011). Defining clear goals, holding schools accountable for meeting the goals, measuring progress, providing support to schools, and removing barriers to effective turnaround practices were identified as critical components of central office leadership by those attending the summit.

Turnaround leadership clearly can be many things, but in the final analysis it boils down to these two essential elements: (1) developing a clear understanding of priorities, and (2) securing broad-based commitment to those priorities. When district leaders are able to identify a focused set of goals for low-performing schools and gain widespread support for achieving the goals, they have accomplished the vital first steps toward academic improvement.

DEVELOPING CAPABLE SCHOOL LEADERS

It takes leadership to develop leadership. Nowhere is this more true than in school districts. Superintendents must recognize when a principal is not providing the leadership needed to turn around a low-performing school. Then they must decide whether there is a strong likelihood that the principal can be trained and coached to become more effective. If not, the prudent course of action is to replace the principal. Such decisions can require a great deal of courage, especially if the principal has been in office for a long time and is popular in the community.

Deborah Jewell-Sherman did not opt to replace principals at first. She reasoned that they should not be blamed because the school district had not provided principals with the training required to tackle a school turnaround. She made provisions to train principals and their leadership teams in how to use data to drive the turnaround process. Only when some principals who received training still failed to measure up did she take steps to replace them.

When the decision is made to replace a principal, district leaders need to understand what qualities are needed for the incoming principal. In chapter 1, I offered some of my opinions regarding important attributes of turn-around principals. Public Impact (2008), an organization involved in helping school districts improve low-performing schools, identifies its own set of four key competencies for turnaround leaders:

1. Driving for results: A strong desire to achieve outstanding results.
2. Influencing for results: The ability to motivate others to achieve results.
3. Problem solving: The ability to analyze data and develop plans that people can follow.
4. Showing confidence to lead: The commitment to stay focused and remain self-assured despite criticism.

Knowing the qualities needed to turn around a low-performing school is one thing. Being able to recruit individuals who possess these qualities is quite another. One study funded by the Thomas B. Fordham Institute (Doyle and Locke, 2014) concluded that large school districts are not doing enough to secure talented school leaders. The report urges districts to provide more attractive compensation packages and take steps to make the job of principal more appealing.

Some school districts offer signing bonuses in order to attract capable turnaround principals. Charlotte-Mecklenburg schools experimented with placing its most successful principals in the lowest-performing schools. The idea was to make it an honor to be assigned to turn around a struggling school. Turnaround principals were publicly recognized as the best of the best and allowed to bring a cadre of staff members with them from their former school.

Once principals have been chosen to lead the turnaround process, they must receive the support needed to succeed. Such support is especially important when the faculty remains largely intact. Allowing principals to bring some trusted individuals from their former school, as was done in Charlotte-Mecklenburg, can be very important. At the very least, an incoming principal should be allowed to constitute a new leadership team. Extra resources with which to supplement the existing faculty, enhance technology, improve the physical plant, and otherwise achieve quick wins also are keys to success. In addition, newly appointed principals need to know that they will have the backing of the superintendent and the human resources department when they seek to remove ineffective faculty members.

Even the most capable turnaround principals are likely to require continuing professional development. Superintendents should make sure that individuals assigned to supervise principals possess the necessary experience and expertise to guide them. A study of successful school turnarounds in North Carolina found that principals benefitted from leadership coaching

(Thompson et al., 2011). Networking with other turnaround principals can be another important source of support. Fairfax County Public Schools established a principal-in-residence program in order for highly regarded veteran principals to be available to mentor new principals.

—◦◦◦—

Turnaround Tip: After taking steps to recruit capable turnaround principals, district leaders must make sure the principals receive the support they need to succeed.

—◦◦◦—

Because the talents required to turn around low-performing schools are in short supply, superintendents may be tempted to move successful turnaround principals to schools that are still struggling. The premature departure of a turnaround principal, however, can be a major setback for a recently turned around school, often leading to a loss of hard-earned gains along with staff and community demoralization. Great caution should be exercised when considering the reassignment of effective turnaround principals.

SUPPORT FOR SCHOOL STAFFING

Building a cohesive and committed faculty is a principal's most important responsibility, but it cannot be accomplished without the support of district leaders. Decisions to hire and remove teachers, for example, ultimately reside with superintendents and school boards. Union contracts also can come into play. Board policies often dictate staffing arrangements and teacher-student ratios. Principals need to work closely with specialists in the district office in order to build and maintain a faculty capable of raising student achievement.

For the lowest-performing schools, the process of building a faculty may begin by replacing significant numbers of teachers. Sometimes current faculty members are required to reapply for their positions, with the proviso that only some individuals will be rehired. In states where collectively bargained contracts govern hiring and placement decisions, superintendents and school boards first may have to renegotiate the contract before radical changes can be made in the staffing of low-performing schools. Rules regarding seniority, for example, may need to be set aside in order to clear the way for hiring the most capable teachers.

When a research group (Lane, Unger, and Rhim, 2013) investigated the impact of faculty reconstitution in Massachusetts schools that were subject to state sanctions because of chronic low achievement, they found that replacing large numbers of teachers had positive effects. In eight of the nine Level 4 (failing) schools that met their achievement targets in Year 1 of the turnaround process, at least half of the teachers were replaced. Level 4 schools that replaced less than a third of their teachers only had a 20 percent success rate.

The districts in which the successful turnaround schools were located in the Massachusetts study all reorganized or revamped their human resources departments in order to improve teacher recruitment and expedite hiring. Allowing low-performing schools to select teachers from the candidate pool *before* other district schools can be an important advantage. Signing bonuses and salary enhancements also increase the likelihood that low-performing schools will secure capable teachers.

In one experiment called the Talent Transfer Initiative, ten school districts paid high-performing elementary teachers an additional $20,000 to transfer to a low-performing school and remain there for at least two years (Sawchuk, 2013). Teams of teachers, rather than individuals, made the switch in each case. Effective teachers already located at the participating schools received an additional $10,000. Students taught by the transfer teachers made greater gains, on average, in both reading and mathematics than their counterparts.

The strategy of transferring teams of highly qualified teachers to low-performing schools is based on the belief that talented educators' impact is amplified when they have the support of other capable peers. Boston and Pittsburgh have embraced this strategy with encouraging results (Ferris, 2012). In Boston, Turnaround Teacher Teams (T3) are made up of teachers with proven track records. T3 teachers constitute at least 25 percent of the teaching staff at the schools to which they are sent, and they typically are assigned to roles as team leaders for a grade level or content area. In Pittsburgh, expert teachers make up the Promise-Readiness Corps (PRC). Groups of six to eight PRC teachers are concentrated within grade-level teams in the ninth and tenth grades. Each team shares a cohort of about one hundred students and moves with the cohort when it advances from the ninth to the tenth grade.

Building a capable faculty is one challenge. Maintaining it is quite another matter. Here, again, district leaders can be of great assistance to principals. By ensuring that special funding is not withdrawn prematurely, they can sustain additional staffing for low-performing schools and prevent teacher-student ratios from growing. District policies that limit midyear teacher transfers help to keep faculties intact. District resources also may be needed to support continuing professional development and professional learning communities.

TECHNICAL SUPPORT AND SUPPLEMENTARY RESOURCES

The knowledge and skills required to turn around a low-performing school are so extensive that it often is necessary to supplement the expertise available in the faculty. Larger school districts have curriculum, instruction, and assessment specialists who can be dispatched to schools to assist with curriculum alignment, instructional improvement, and development of common assessments. Other specialists from central offices provide help with technology integration, data analysis, and planning.

Recall the efforts made by Yvonne Brandon to support the turnaround of schools in Richmond. Decisions regarding curriculum content, instructional methods, and assessments were centralized. Central office staff carefully researched new programs before purchasing them. Programs had to be scientifically based, possess embedded assessments, and provide for continuous professional development in order to be considered. Brandon also insisted that vendors with whom the district contracted had to become ongoing partners in the turnaround process. Richmond had no need for outfits that delivered materials and departed.

In order for assistance to be truly helpful, coordination across vendors and district specialists is essential. Flooding a low-performing school with outside experts who have not worked out a carefully coordinated plan of assistance actually can set back the turnaround process (Duke and Landahl, 2011). Teachers become confused when they receive conflicting advice from various sources. District leaders must insist that vendors and district specialists determine how they plan to help school-based educators *before* they descend on a school.

Some school systems may be so small or disorganized that they are unable to provide the technical assistance needed by low-performing schools. In these instances, arranging to work with a *lead partner* can be a viable alternative. Since the advent of school turnaround initiatives in 2002, dozens of organizations have developed programs for helping to train turnaround principals and teachers and for guiding the development and implementation of School

Turnaround Plans. The costs of contracting with lead partners often can be covered by School Improvement Grants, state funds, and grants from private foundations. Not all potential lead partners, however, are equally capable of addressing local needs, so it is essential for district leaders to review each lead partner's track record, offerings, and financial stability.

That schools designated for turnaround require resources over and above those normally budgeted has already been noted. These resources may be needed for additional teachers, full-time specialists and coaches, extended learning time and longer school years, special programs and materials, assessments, transportation, summer programs, and so on. District leaders charged with developing and overseeing school budgets should make certain that the additional funds for launching a school turnaround are not withdrawn prematurely, thereby jeopardizing early gains. The forementioned study of successful turnarounds in North Carolina recommended at least three years of additional funding in order to secure early gains (Thompson et al., 2011).

RESTRUCTURING TO FACILITATE DISTRICT SUPPORT SERVICES

Some of the key ways that district leaders support school turnaround initiatives have been discussed already—recruitment and selection of capable principals and teachers, ongoing professional development, additional funding, technical support, and arrangements with lead partners. These functions are just the beginning, however. District personnel may be involved in monitoring School Turnaround Plans, managing contracts with vendors and lead partners, keeping parents and the community informed about how turnaround efforts are progressing, communicating with state and federal officials responsible for overseeing turnaround schools, and accounting for the expenditure of funds.

School districts with more than a couple of low-performing schools are finding that there are benefits to clustering these schools under the auspices of a special unit devoted solely to the supervision and coordination of turnaround initiatives. The Educational Transformation Office for the Miami-Dade school system, the nation's fourth largest district, is responsible, for example, for 108 low-performing schools (as of 2014). Assigning responsibility to one unit and its designated leader eliminates duplication of effort and increases the likelihood of timely and focused assistance for schools.

—⊷—

Turnaround Tip: Districts with a number of low-performing schools can benefit from creating a special unit devoted exclusively to supervising and coordinating turnaround efforts.

—⊷—

Mass Insight, a nonprofit organization that offers assistance to school systems engaged in school turnaround, developed a helpful manual for districts interested in creating a special unit to oversee turnaround efforts (Mass Insight, 2010). Five basic responsibilities were outlined for District Turnaround Offices (DTOs). They include attracting and supporting partners, coordinating school support, fostering human capital, monitoring and oversight, and securing resources.

The manual goes on to list key factors for the successful operation of DTOs. It is recommended, for instance, that the executive in charge of the DTO report directly to the superintendent and possess the authority to make decisions without having to go through lots of bureaucratic channels. The resources available to the DTO should be clearly spelled out. Regular channels of communication between the DTO and turnaround schools should be established. The recruitment of talented individuals to staff the DTO and provide services to turnaround schools must be a high priority.

Small school districts may not be able to afford a separate unit for supervising and coordinating turnaround efforts, but they at least should consider assigning one district official responsibility for leading turnaround efforts and keeping the superintendent and school board apprised of progress.

The message in this chapter, as in the previous chapters, is straightforward. Low-performing schools do not improve because of good intentions alone. Sustainable turnarounds demand focused leadership at all levels, from the classroom to the principal's office to the district office. Instructional expertise, continuous data-based planning, and additional resources also are essential elements. Knowing the ingredients necessary to raise student achievement does not make the hard work of school turnaround any easier, but it does mean that there is reason to be hopeful.

NOTE

1. The material concerning Deborah Jewell-Sherman's efforts to turn around Richmond Public Schools was drawn from an unpublished case study written by the author and Michael Salmonowicz for the University of Virginia's Partnership for Leaders in Education.

REFERENCES

Doyle, D. and Locke, G. 2014. *Lacking Leaders: The Challenges of Principal Recruitment, Selection, and Placement.* Washington, DC: Thomas B. Fordham Institute.

Duke, D. L. and Landahl, M. 2011. "Raising test scores was the easy part": A case study of the third year of school turnaround. *International Studies in Educational Administration,* 39(3), 91–114.

Ferris, K. 2012. Human capital in turnaround schools. *School Administrator,* 7(69), 36–39.

Lane, B.; Unger, C.; and Rhim, L. M. 2013. *Emerging and Sustaining Practices for School Turnaround.* Baltimore, MD: Institute for Strategic Leadership and Learning.

Mass Insight. 2010. The District Turnaround Office: A Comprehensive Support Structure for Struggling Schools. Boston: Mass Insight.

Public Impact. 2008. School turnaround leaders: Competencies for success. Downloaded at http://publicimpact.com/teachers-leaders/competencies-of-high-performers.

Sawchuk, S. November 13, 2013. Transferring top teachers has benefits. *Education Week,* 33(12), 1,13.

Sustaining School Turnaround at Scale. 2011. Watertown, MA: Education Resource Strategies.

Thompson, C. L.; Brown, K. M.; Townsend, L. W.; Henry, G. T.; and Fortner, C. K. 2011. *Turning Around North Carolina's Lowest Achieving Schools (2006–2010).* Chapel Hill, NC: Consortium for Educational Research and Evaluation—North Carolina.

Last Words

Windmills. Wishing wells. Wings. Each could be a metaphor for the school turnaround process. For some, turning around a low-performing school is a Quixotic quest, akin to tilting at windmills. For others, the undertaking is little different from throwing money into a wishing well and hoping for the best. When I think of school turnarounds, however, the image of wings comes to mind. Successful turnarounds lift low-performing schools, allowing students to take flight in search of meaningful lives.

If you are a principal or a prospective principal of a low-performing school and you question how much can actually be done to raise achievement, please reconsider. Don't determine the importance of turnaround leadership based solely on standardized test data and the calculations of nameless number crunchers in remote offices. Instead, judge the worth of leading a low-performing school in terms of a different measure. I call it the never-give-up criterion.

If you can say at the end of each school day that you did not give up on any child in your care, that you continued to search for ways to reach and help every struggling student, no matter how much they resisted assistance, then you deserve to look in the mirror and tell yourself that you have made an extraordinary contribution to the welfare of your society. Educators cannot guarantee that every student will learn all that they are expected to learn any more than parents can guarantee that their children will turn out to be model citizens. As educators, however, we have a professional and an ethical obligation never to stop trying to help each and every student learn as much as they can in the time they have with us.

Index

Stuart High School (Fairfax County, VA), 99

student absenteeism: *see* attendance

student achievement, 13, 95, 96, 102, 151, 158, 161–65, 167, 169, 171, 173, 174, 179, 180, 183, 184–85, 189, 190–91, 195, 197, 199; causes of low achievement, 2, 25–27, 29, 39–62, 102, 140, 176; data, 24, 29–36, 95, 140, 170; high achievers, 107; predictors, 59–60; school-based causes, 2, 26–27, 30, 68, 102

student behavior, 5, 12, 34–36, 102–3, 125, 163, 190; academic behaviors, 35–36, 115–19; data, 34–36, 190; interventions, 102–3, 146

student grouping, 52, 106, 122, 128, 131, 162, 164, 169, 171, 197

student health, 104

student involvement in school turnaround, 51, 60, 65, 147, 148, 151, 157–58

student work habits, 5, 35–36, 93, 115–19

succession planning, 175

summer school, 96, 98, 124, 131, 191, 197, 205

sustainability (of school turnaround), 167–87, 189, 198–99

Taft Information Technology High School (Cincinnati, OH), 183

Talent Transfer Initiative, 203

teacher: evaluation, 46; leaders, 94–95, 168–69, 174, 175, 176, 203; mentors, 176; planning, 50, 97–98; recruitment,

105, 141, 176, 203; retention, 91, 105–6, 108, 176; selection, 141, 176, 203; specialists, 12, 45–47, 100, 107, 120, 121, 123, 137, 164, 169–70, 198, 205; turnover, 1, 45, 46, 91, 93, 108, 141, 173, 176, 177

Texas Turnaround Leadership Academy, 7

theory of action (for school turnaround), 26–28

Thomas, Catherine, 93–94

Title I, 63, 91, 164, 170

troubleshooting, 6, 171, 173, 183–85

trust, 12, 100, 104–5, 143–44, 175, 182

turnaround diagnostics, 5, 26–27, 29–36, 39–62, 69; external causes of low-achievement, 26–27, 42–44, 58, 173; school-based causes of low achievement, 2, 26–27, 30, 42, 44–55, 58, 68, 173

turnaround principal qualifications, 18–21, 200–1

turnaround teacher teams, 203

tutoring, 97, 120, 124, 163–64, 168, 170, 183

University of Virginia School Turnaround Specialist Program, 10, 67, 91, 93, 198–99

Voyager reading program, 191, 197

Warren, Nancy, 146–47

Weisskopf, Nancy, 51, 94, 97, 107, 113, 126, 127, 142, 147, 157–58, 181

writing instruction, 164, 180

About the Author

After teaching high school social studies and serving as a secondary school administrator, **Daniel L. Duke** embarked on a career in higher education. For four decades he has taught courses on educational leadership, organizational change, and school reform as well as conducting research on various aspects of public schools. After serving on the faculties of Lewis and Clark College and Stanford University, he came to the University of Virginia as chair of educational leadership and policy studies. Duke founded and directed the Thomas Jefferson Center for Educational Design and helped establish the Darden-Curry Partnership for Leaders in Education (PLE), a unique enterprise involving the Curry School of Education and the Darden Graduate School of Business Administration. He served as research director for the PLE until 2010.

A prolific writer, Duke has authored or co-authored thirty-two books and several hundred scholarly articles, monographs, chapters, and reports. His most recent books include *The Challenges of Education Change* (2004), *Education Empire: The Evolution of an Excellent Suburban School System* (2005), *Teachers' Guide to School Turnarounds* (2007), *The Little School System that Could: Transforming a City School District* (2008), *Differentiating School Leadership* (2010), and *The Challenges of School District Leadership* (2010).

A highly regarded consultant, Duke has worked with over 150 school systems, state agencies, foundations, and governments across the United States
and abroad. Recently he helped develop the Texas Turnaround Leadership
Academy and the Florida Turnaround Leaders Program. He has served as
president of the University Council for Educational Administration and was
chosen as Professor of the Year at the Curry School of Education.